The Early Years

companion volumes

The School Years
Assessing and Promoting Resilience in Vulnerable Children 2
Brigid Daniel and Sally Wassell
ISBN 1 84310 018 5

Adolescence
Assessing and Promoting Resilience in Vulnerable Children 3
Brigid Daniel and Sally Wassell
ISBN 1 84310 019 3

Set of three workbooks
ISBN 1 84310 045 2

of related interest

Child Development for Child Care and Protection Workers
Brigid Daniel, Sally Wassell and Robbie Gilligan
ISBN 1 85302 633 6

The Child's World
Assessing Children in Need
Edited by Jan Horwath
ISBN 1 85302 957 2

Approaches to Needs Assessment in Children's Services
Edited by Harriet Ward and Wendy Rose
ISBN 1 85302 780 4

Social Work with Children and Families
Getting into Practice
Ian Butler and Gwenda Roberts
ISBN 1 85302 365 5

Creating a Safe Place
Helping Children and Families Recover from Child Sexual Abuse
NCH Children and Families Project
ISBN 1 84310 009 6

The Early Years

Assessing and Promoting Resilience in Vulnerable Children 1

Brigid Daniel and Sally Wassell
Illustrated by Iain Campbell

Jessica Kingsley Publishers
London and Philadelphia

First published in the United Kingdom in 2002
by Jessica Kingsley Publishers
116 Pentonville Road
London N1 9JB, UK
and
400 Market Street, Suite 400
Philadelphia, PA 19106, USA

www.jkp.com

Library of Congress Cataloging in Publication Data
Daniel, Brigid, 1959-
    Assessing and promoting resilence in vulnerable children/Brigid Daniel and Sally
Wassell ; illustrated by Iain Campbell.
        p. Cm.
    Includes bibliographical references.
    Contents: 1. The early years -- 2. The school years -- 3. Adolescence.
    ISBN 1-84310-013-4 (v. 1 : alk. paper) -- ISBN 1-84310-018-5 (v. 2 : alk. paper) --
ISBN 1-84310-019-3 (v. 3 : alk. Paper)
    1. Children with social disabilities. 2. Teenagers with social disabilities. 3. Resilience
(Personality trait) in children. 4. Resilience (Personality trait) in adolescence. 5. Social
work with children. 6. Social work with teenagers. I. Wassell, Sally. II. Title.
HV713 .D36 2002
362.7--dc21
                                                                                        2002027536

British Library Cataloguing in Publication Data
A CIP catalogue record for this book is available from the British Library

ISBN-13: 978 1 84310 013 3
ISBN-10: 1 84310 013 4

Printed and Bound in Great Britain by
Athenaeum Press, Gateshead, Tyne and Wear

Contents

Acknowledgements   7

1   Introduction to Resilience   9

    Domains of Resilience   14

    Summary of Factors Associated with Resilience
       during Early Years   15

2   When and How to Use the Workbook   17

Part I Assessment

3   Secure Base   27

    Secure Base Checklist: Child   30

    Secure Base Checklist: Parent/Carer   32

    Quality of Attachment   34

4   Education   35

    Education Checklist: Child   38

    Education Checklist: Parent/Carer   40

5   Friendships   42

    Friendships Checklist: Child   45

    Friendships Checklist: Parent/Carer   47

6   Talents and Interests   49

    Talents and Interests Checklist: Child   52

    Talents and Interests Checklist: Parent/Carer   54

7   Positive Values   56

        Positive Values Checklist: Child   60
        Emotional Faces   62
        Theory of Mind   64
        Emotional Scenes   65
        Positive Values Checklist: Parent/Carer   70

8   Social Competencies   72

        Social Competencies Checklist: Child   75
        Social Attributes Checklist   78
        Social Competencies Checklist: Parent/Carer   80

Part II Intervention

9   Intervention Strategies   85

        Practice Suggestions: Secure Base   87
        Practice Suggestions: Education   97
        Practice Suggestions: Friendships   102
        Practice Suggestions: Talents and Interests   104
        Practice Suggestions: Positive Values   110
        Practice Suggestions: Social Competencies   113

10 Case Studies   119

        David, aged 4   119
        Susan, aged 3   121

    Appendix: Moral Reasoning Stages   124

    Bibliography   127

    Subject Index   131

    Author Index   135

Acknowledgements

The writing and production of these workbooks was financially supported by the Social Work Services Inspectorate of the Scottish Executive. We would like to thank practitioners who helped to develop the material in these workbooks from Perth Social Work Department, Maryhill Social Work Centre, Glasgow and Children's Centres in North Edinburgh. We would also like to thank Robbie Gilligan, Professor of Social Work and Social Policy, and Director, Children's Research Centre, Trinity College, Dublin, and Jim Ennis, Elaine Ennis and Amelia Wilson of the Centre for Child Care and Protection Studies, Department of Social Work, University of Dundee for conceptual development and Helen Wosu for detailed comments. We are also extremely grateful to Stacey Farmer for administrative support. Thanks also to Christine Henderson and David Willshaw for support and encouragement.

Some of the issues in the workbooks have previously been published in Daniel, B., Wassell, S. and Gilligan, R. (1999) '"It's just common sense isn't it?": Exploring ways of putting the theory of resilience into action.' *Adoption and Fostering 23* 3, 6–15 and are reproduced with the permission of British Agencies for Adoption and Fostering (BAAF). The table of Kohlberg's stages of moral development has been reproduced from Schaffer, H. R. (1996) *Social Development* with the permission of Blackwell Publishers Inc.

1
Introduction to Resilience

Ecological framework

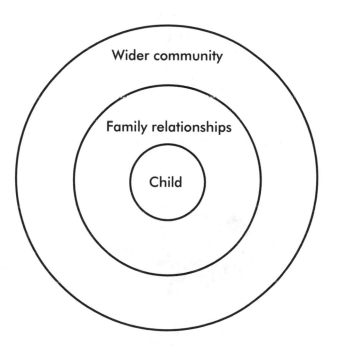

Figure 1.1 Three ecological levels at which resilience factors can be located

Throughout these workbooks the practitioner is encouraged to place assessment and intervention practice within an ecological framework (Brofenbrenner 1989). This entails considering what resources might be available to the child at each of three levels (see Figure 1.1):

1. the individual, for example, in dispositional and temperamental attributes

2. close family or substitute family relationships, for example, in secure attachments

3. the wider community, for example, in extrafamilial supports.

All the checklists will address aspects of each of these levels and suggestions for intervention will be provided for different ecological levels.

Resilience

Resilience can be defined as: 'Normal development under difficult conditions' (Fonagy *et al.* 1994).

Due to a wide range of practice and theoretical research, the protective factors that support positive outcomes, despite adversity, are becoming better understood (Rutter 1985; Werner 1990; Werner and Smith 1992). These protective factors that are associated with long-term social and emotional well-being have been located at all levels of the child's ecological social environment. The existence of protective factors can help explain why one child may cope better with adverse life events than another.

Figure 1.2 Dimension on which individual resilience can be located

The level of individual resilience can be seen as falling on a dimension of resilience and vulnerability (see Figure 1.2).

This dimension is usually used to refer to intrinsic qualities of an individual. Some children are more intrinsically resilient than others because of a whole range of factors that will be detailed later (Werner and Smith 1992). For example, an 'easy' temperament is associated with resilience in infancy.

A further dimension for the understanding of individual differences is that of protective and adverse environments; this dimension covers extrinsic factors and is therefore located at the outer ecological levels of family and wider community.

Figure 1.3 Dimension on which factors of resilience around the child can be located

Examples of protective factors are the existence of a close attachment and the presence of a supportive extended family member (see Figure 1.3).

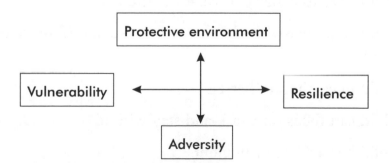

Figure 1.4 Framework for the assessment of resilience factors

When considered together these dimensions provide a framework for the assessment of adverse and positive factors at all ecological levels of a child's socio-emotional environment (Daniel, Wassell and Gilligan 1999) (see Figure 1.4).

The two dimensions will interact: an increase in protective factors will help to boost a child's individual resilience. Therefore, the workbook encourages the assessment of potential protective factors at each ecological level, with the aim of building up protective factors and thus boosting resilience.

Resilience is a complex issue and some caution is required. For example, it can be possible for children to appear to be coping well with adversity, whereas in fact they may be internalising their symptoms (Luthar 1991). Apparent coping cannot be taken at face value and careful, wide-ranging assessment is essential.

The assessment of resilience is not straightforward: the vast majority of studies have been carried out retrospectively. However, a number of checklists have been devised that aim to measure levels of resilience. For example, the International Resilience Project uses a simple checklist of 15 items that indicate resilience in a child (Grotberg 1997, p.20):

1. The child has someone who loves him/her totally (unconditionally).

2. The child has an older person outside the home she/he can tell about problems and feelings.

3. The child is praised for doing things on his/her own.

4. The child can count on her/his family being there when needed.

5. The child knows someone he/she wants to be like.

6. The child believes things will turn out all right.

7. The child does endearing things that make people like her/him.

8. The child believes in power greater than seen.

9. The child is willing to try new things.

10. The child likes to achieve in what he/she does.

11. The child feels that what she/he does makes a difference in how things come out.

12. The child likes himself/herself.

13. The child can focus on a task and stay with it.

14. The child has a sense of humour.

15. The child makes plans to do things.

Although many factors can be associated with resilience, there appear to be three fundamental building blocks that underpin them (Gilligan 1997):

1. A secure base, whereby the child feels a sense of belonging and security.

2. Good self-esteem, that is, an internal sense of worth and competence.

3. A sense of self-efficacy, that is, a sense of mastery and control, along with an accurate understanding of personal strengths and limitations.

These workbooks cover six domains of a child's life that will contribute to each of these three building blocks of resilience.

Because resilience is associated with better long-term outcomes, it can be used as a guiding principle when planning for children whose lives have been disrupted by abuse and or neglect and who may require to be looked after away from home (Gilligan 1997). Indeed:

> Resilience – the capacity to transcend adversity – may be seen as the essential quality which care planning and provision should seek to stimulate as a key outcome of the care offered. (Gilligan 1997, p.14)

When the home life of a child is disrupted for whatever reason, considerable attention is rightly paid to the issue of attachment and to placement, either in supporting the child to live at home or in the provision of an appropriate alternative home life. However, whatever the arrangements for the day-to-day care of such children, attention can also be paid to fostering their resilience. This approach recognises that although it may not always be possible to protect children from further adversity, and that while it may not always be possible to provide an ideal environment for them, boosting their resilience should enhance the likelihood of a better long-term outcome.

A resilience-based approach focuses on maximising the likelihood of a better outcome for children by building a protective network around them. The concept of resilience increasingly offers an alternative framework for intervention, the focus being on the assessment of potential areas of strength within the child's whole system. As yet, there is very little research into proactive attempts to promote resilience.

Whatever arrangements are made for the care of the child, this approach offers social workers a real focus for positive practice. This approach enables a move away from an assumption that a parent or alternative placement will provide all that the child needs. Instead the emphasis is on building a network of support from the resources available, and adding to them with professional support where necessary. It also emphasises the importance of building on the potential areas of resilience within the child, for example, by maximising opportunities for engaging in hobbies, associating with friends, experiencing success, making a contribution and so on. What is important is that practitioners have the theoretical grounding that assures them that they can make a difference to the outcomes for children with such measures, even if they never see the results themselves. This assurance should help to reduce feelings of powerlessness and purposelessness.

DOMAINS OF RESILIENCE

Figure 1.5 Six domains of resilience

Throughout the workbooks aspects of resilience in six domains will be considered (see Figure 1.5).

Factors within each of these domains of a child's life, at each of the three ecological levels, are known to contribute to a child's level of vulnerability or resilience to adversity such as abuse, neglect and loss. More detail will be provided about each domain in the relevant section below.

It will be noted that these domains are similar to, but not identical with, the dimensions used in the Looking After Children (LAC) materials (Parker *et al.* 1991). However, much of the information required to assess resilience will be contained in completed LAC materials. The seven LAC dimensions can be linked with the six domains of resilience as follows:

1. Health: secure base

2. Education: education

3. Emotional and behavioural development: secure base/friendships/positive values

4. Family and peer relationships: secure base/friendships

5. Self-care and competence: secure base/social competencies

6. Identity: talents and interests

7. Social presentation: social competencies.

SUMMARY OF FACTORS ASSOCIATED WITH RESILIENCE DURING EARLY YEARS

Individual factors associated with resilience

- female

- first-born

- no birth complications

- full term

- easy sleeping and feeding

- affectionate

- drive and vigour

- socially responsive

- actively reaches for others

- secure attachment

- advanced in communication and so on

- alert and cheerful

- adaptable

- fearless

- seeks out novel experiences.

Family factors associated with resilience

- close bond with at least one person

- nurturance and trust

- lack of separations

- lack of parental mental health or addiction problems

- close grandparents

- family harmony

- sibling attachment

- four or fewer children

- sufficient financial and material resources.

Wider community factors associated with resilience

- neighbour and other non-kin support

- peer contact

- good nursery experience.

2

When and How to Use
the Workbook

When?

These workbooks are intended as an aid to planning purposeful intervention with
children and young people (see Figure 2.1). They are to be used in conjunction with
Looking After Children materials when carrying out a comprehensive assessment of

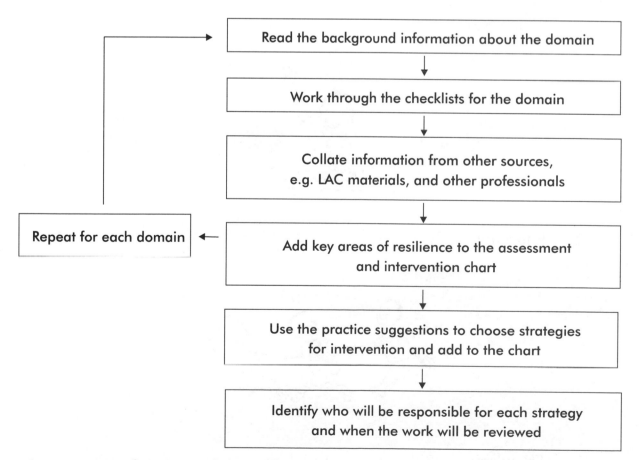

Figure 2.1 Process of assessment and planning for intervention

need; they can also be used to provide a baseline assessment against which the efficacy of intervention can be evaluated. They can be used to aid planning for children and young people living at home and for those living away from home.

How?

Ensure that you have chosen the appropriate workbook from one of three:

1.   Pre-school children (early years)

2.   School-age children

3.   Adolescents.

The workbook takes you through a process of assessment for each of the six domains:

1.   Secure base

2.   Education

3.   Friendships

4.   Talents and interests

5.   Positive values

6.   Social competencies.

Child checklist

When using the child's checklist try, as much as possible, to involve the child directly in the process. Explain what you are trying to find out and cover each of the points in the checklists with the child. Reword as appropriate. Try to arrange as much direct observation of behaviour as possible.

Parent/carer checklist

Go through the parent/carer checklist with any significant parent or carer. If there are significant differences between different people's responses, then explore this with the respondents and aim to reach a consensus on areas to work on.

A decision will need to be made for each situation as to whether to concentrate on an assessment of parental environment or carer environment. When the aim is for the child to stay at or return home, the focus may need to be upon home environment. If the child is to be accommodated on a long-term basis away from home, then the focus may need to be upon assessment of carer environment with a view to looking for aspects that might help with boosting resilience.

Use the checklists as a guide only, gather information from as wide a range of sources as possible, particularly from the LAC materials, and try to involve the child as much as possible, taking account of age and stage of development.

Assessment

Once you have assessed a domain, identify areas of actual or potential resilience at any ecological level that could be targeted for intervention and note them on the assessment and intervention chart. The assessment process is completed by bringing the information from each of the six domains together onto the chart.

Intervention

The workbook then takes you through a process of planning intervention. Look through the intervention strategies for each domain and use them to help plan strategies for the targeted areas for intervention. Note the strategies onto the assessment and intervention chart. In consultation with key people in the child's life, identify who will be responsible for each strategy. Remember to consider the informal network as well as professionals.

Evaluation

Ensure that a plan for evaluation and ongoing monitoring is built into the strategy for intervention and note this onto the assessment and intervention chart.

Please remember:

1. One social worker cannot do it all. Aim to develop a network of formal and informal supports around the child.

2. Look at existing, mainstream community resources.

3. Try to balance intervention that aims to build on existing strengths, with strategies for boosting less strong areas.

4. Positive effects in one domain can spill over to another, the domains should therefore not be viewed as independent and separate, but as interactive and dynamic.

Assessment and intervention chart

Domain	What areas of resilience, at any ecological level, will we target now?	How will we do this?	Who will be responsible for this?	How and when will we measure progress?
Secure base				
Education				

The Early Years, © Brigid Daniel and Sally Wassell 2002 © Iain Campbell 2002

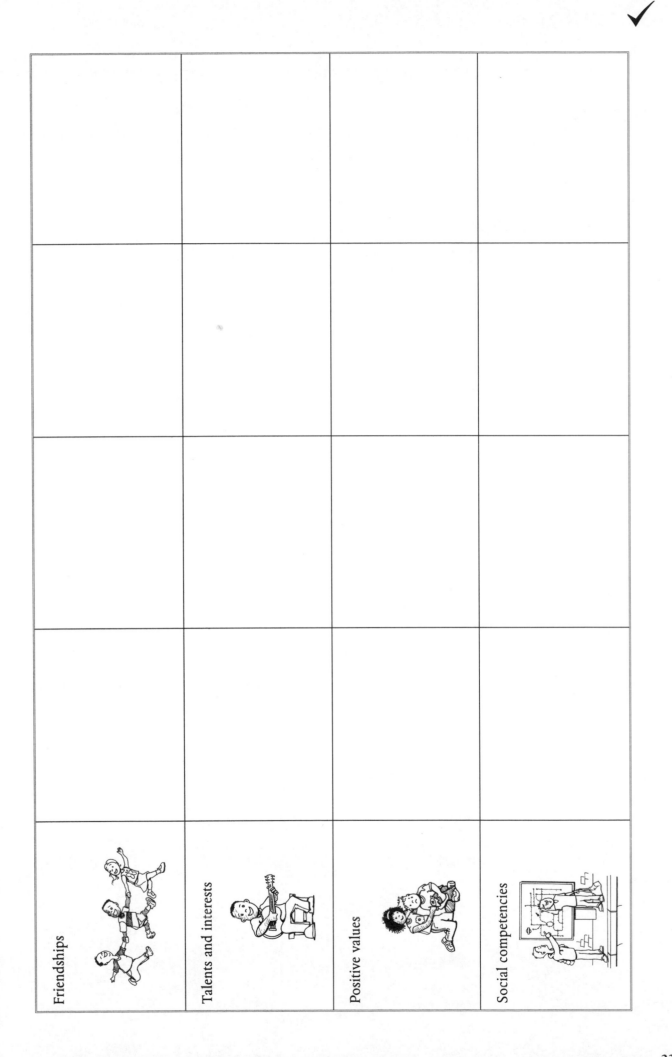

Friendships			
Talents and interests			
Positive values			
Social competencies			

Part I

Assessment

3

Secure Base

Background information

There is a clear association between the presence of a secure attachment relationship and resilience in the face of adversity (Werner 1990). The importance of attachment ties has been recognised in child-care practice for many years and normally underpins planning (Daniel *et al.* 1999; Fahlberg 1991; Howe 1995; Howe *et al.* 1999). It is during early years that the foundations of attachment are laid down. The classic studies to demonstrate attachment behaviour are normally carried out with toddlers (Ainsworth *et al.* 1978). These studies have shown that attachment behaviours can fall into one of several distinctive patterns. The most important distinction is between *secure* and *insecure* attachment. Young children who are classified as showing *secure* attachment play happily when their care-giver is present, protest when they leave and go to them for comfort on their return. They will show some wariness of strangers and choose their care-giver for comfort when upset or fearful. What they have is a base that not only is stable, but also acts as a springboard to the wider social world. Long-term resilience is associated with the opportunity to develop a secure attachment to at least one person.

During the development of secure attachment the child may show some fear of strangers between 6 and 16 months, and anxiety at separation from the attachment figure between about 7 and 24 months.

Children who are classified as *insecure* may show one of four patterns.

1. If *avoidant* they tend to shun the care-giver after a separation and appear not to discriminate markedly in their behaviour towards a stranger and their care-giver.

2. If *ambivalent* they appear to want comfort from the care-giver after a separation, but at the same time show resistance to comfort, for example by squirming out of a hug.

3. A further form of insecure attachment, known as *disorganised*, is demonstrated in a mixture of reactions where the child appears confused and unable to feel comforted by the care-giver. Children who have been abused or neglected are more likely to show insecure patterns of attachment.

4. Another pattern of insecure attachment has been identified by Downes (1992) that is characterised by an *anxious preoccupation* with the availability of the carer. It is a pattern that can often be encountered in practice with abused and neglected children.

Secure attachment is associated with a parenting style that is warm and sensitive. The parent has to be able to take account of the child's needs and temperament and respond appropriately. Patterns of attachment are, therefore, the products of a *relationship* between the child and the adult, and are influenced by the interaction between the child (with his or her temperament) and the adult. The early pattern of attachment acts as a kind of template or internal working model for later relationships. The internal working model is, therefore, based upon the child's sense of self and his or her experience of others. Howe *et al.* (1999, p.25) summarise it in the following way:

Self (loved, effective, autonomous and competent) + other people (available, cooperative and dependable) = *secure* attachment patterns.

Self (unloved but self-reliant) + other people (rejecting and intrusive) = *avoidant* attachment patterns.

Self (low value, ineffective and dependent) + other people (neglecting, insensitive, unpredictable and unreliable) + *ambivalent* attachment patterns.

Self (confused and bad) + other people (frightening and unavailable) = *disorganised* attachment patterns.

An important factor in the attachment relationship is the parent's own attachment history and the meaning it has for him or her. The way that adults talk about their own attachment experiences provides insight into their own level of security. Adults whose experience was of an abusive or neglectful childhood need not themselves be insecure. They can be considered secure if they have had an opportunity to process their experiences and can recount those experiences in a coherent way that suggests that they can make sense of their past (Main and Weston 1981). Having the opportunity and ability to reflect upon attachment experiences is key to overcoming difficult or disturbing past circumstances (Fonargy et al. 1994). It is also important to consider the ways in which current circumstances might undermine parents' ability to be sensitive to their child's needs, such as a difficult relationship with a partner, poverty, poor housing, social isolation and so on.

Children may have a secure relationship with one person (for example, the father) and insecure with another (for example, the mother), therefore the quality of all important relationships must be assessed (Fox, Kimmerly and Scafer 1991). The aim in practice is to ensure that children are provided with a secure base, either by improving the relationship with the parent/s or, if necessary, by finding an alternative attachment figure. Insecure internal working models of attachment can change in the context of the formation of new, more secure relationships (Feeney and Noffer 1996). Therefore, for younger children particularly, this can be a fruitful area of intervention. When it is not immediately possible to enable the attachment to one person, a network of attachment figures can be created around the child.

It may be possible to enhance the protective network by considering contact with family members, including absent fathers, siblings and extended family. It is also important to find out who is important to the child now and how to make use of current attachments. Resilience theory would suggest an emphasis on building a protective network of support from all the resources available, and adding to them with professional support where necessary.

SECURE BASE CHECKLIST
CHILD

In a thorough and comprehensive text, Howe *et al.* (1999) set out detailed guidance for the assessment of patterns of attachment and the planning of intervention. If initial assessment suggests attachment problems to be the key issue then we would recommend that you consult this book for more information. They suggest that assessment must include making inquiries of the files and the wider professional network, observing children in various circumstances, and interviewing parents and children.

There needs to be a decision about which attachment relationships to assess. It is recommended that if the child is living at home then an assessment be carried out on all significant adults, whether resident in the house or not, for example, mother, father, grandparent. If the child is living away from home then the relationship with the carer or keyworker should be assessed, as well as any continuing family relationships. The following checklists should therefore be used flexibly and be adjusted according to requirements.

Does this child appear to feel secure?

1. Observe the child in a range of settings. Look at how he or she deals with stress and distress, at how he or she relates to adults and other children and at how willing the child is to explore the environment. From such observations it should be possible to build up a picture of the child's general level of security.

2. Reflect upon the way that the child relates to you and other adults. Do you feel that the child shows a healthy discrimination between known and unknown adults?

3. From the information in the files and from any other source, compile a detailed list of any significant losses or separations that this child has experienced.

Does the current parent or carer environment provide the child with a secure base?

1. Observe the interaction between the child and each significant adult. Use the observations of the verbal and non-verbal aspects of the relationship and the consistency and sensitivity of the adult response to the child to gauge the quality of the attachment relationship.

2. Is there a predictable routine of care?

3. Observe the child at times of separation from, and reunion with, significant adults. Does the child show a healthy pattern of separation or are there signs of over-anxiety, clinginess or indifference?

4. At times of distress can the child be comforted by significant adults?

5. Is the parent or carer able to make time for the child?

6. If the child is living away from home, does he or she have contact with a parent and is the purpose for that contact clear?

What are the wider resources that contribute to the child's attachment network?

1. Create an ecomap using circles to represent the child and any other person who is, or who has been, important to the child, including other children. Map the child's network, with the person who is most important to the child closest to him or her. The older children in this age group should be able to help with this activity.

2. Does the parent have adequate emotional and material resources to support him or her in the parenting of the child?

3. What informal human resources are available within the child's network? Does the child have an extended family network, and is there someone who may be able to offer time to this child?

4. Does the child attend a nursery or some form of day-care provision? If not are there such resources available in the locality?

SECURE BASE CHECKLIST
PARENT/CARER

Does this child appear to feel secure?

Ask the parent/carer:

1. What does this child do if upset? How does he or she show their distress and show that they want comfort?

2. How willing is he or she to explore new places, toys and so on?

3. Does he or she react differently to unknown adults from how he or she reacts to known adults?

4. What significant losses or separations has this child experienced?

Does the current parent or carer environment provide the child with a secure base?

1. Ask the parent about his or her own experiences of loss, separation and rejection; experiences of emotional upsets, hurts and sickness and his or her experiences of love and acceptance with their parents or carers. Consider the nature of the account. Is he or she able to provide a clear, coherent and considered description of his or her own experiences? Does it appear that he or she would benefit from an opportunity to reflect upon his or her attachment history?

2. Use the quality of attachment measure (devised by Lucy Berliner and David Fine). It is perhaps more appropriate for slightly older children, but may be helpful for the assessment of pre-school children.

Ask the parent/carer:

1. What do you think the relationship between you and the child is like? Is it as you would like it to be, or are there aspects that worry you? (If it may be of help, describe the different patterns of attachment to the parent.)

2. What is your routine of care? (For example, mealtimes, bath times etc.)

3. What happens when you and the child separate? Does he or she show signs of over-anxiety, clinginess or indifference?

4. What do you usually do to comfort the child when he or she is distressed? Does this usually work?

5. Do you find that you can make time for your child?

6. (If the child is living away from home) do you feel that you have enough contact with your child? What do you understand the reason for the contact to be?

What are the wider resources that contribute to the child's attachment network?

Ask the parent/carer:

1. Could you name all the people (adult or child) that the child knows, or has known in the past, who you think are important to him or her?

2. Do you feel that you have enough support to be able to be a good parent? Is there anything that you think makes it difficult to parent, for example, lack of money, poor housing, lack of friends, lack of educational opportunities and so on?

3. Can you think of anybody that you know who may be able to spend some time with your child?

4. If the child does not attend a nursery or some form of day-care provision, do you think this would be of benefit?

✓

QUALITY OF ATTACHMENT

This tool has been developed by Lucy Berliner and David Fine, Center for Sexual Assault and Traumatic Stress, Harborview Medical Center, Seattle, Washington and is reproduced with their permission. The process of detailed evaluation and validation of this material is currently underway. Modified versions may therefore be produced in the future.

Four short descriptions are provided which relate to each of the four types of attachment:

- secure attachment (Type B)

- insecure – avoidant (Type A)

- insecure – ambivalent (Type C)

- insecure – disorganised (Type D)

Simply ask the parent or carer to say which description best fits the child's attachment behaviour.

Child/adolescent smiles, and often seeks physical contact when greeting you; having you present relaxes child; s/he is usually comfortable when alone or separated from you. (B)

Child/adolescent appears independent, almost too independent for their age; s/he may avoid you; s/he is not upset at separation; child/adolescent is as comfortable with strangers as family members. (A)

Child/adolescent is clingy and anxious with you; gets upset when separated from you and may have difficulty being alone; s/he is glad to see you, but at the same time may act angry or upset. (C)

Child/adolescent may show a mixture of being distant and anxious; s/he can be angry and controlling or be compliant, but in an overly sweet/fake way. (D)

4

Education

Background information

Good educational attainment is associated with good outcomes and is therefore a protective factor that should be aimed for (Rutter 1991). School or pre-school provision also offers a wide range of other opportunities to boost resilience, including acting as a complementary secure base, providing many opportunities for developing self-esteem and efficacy and opportunities for constructive contact with peers and supportive adults (Garbarino *et al.* 1992; Gilligan 1998).

There may be a temptation for practitioners to concentrate on issues of attachment with young children. However, when a child is unsettled intellectual development cannot be suspended: the early years are so vital for cognitive development that it must always be a priority for attention.

Children's early cognitive development is described as moving through the *sensorimotor* stage where they have no mental representation of events to the *pre-operational* stage when internal representations are beginning and can be seen in the use of language and make-believe. Piaget (1952) described children at these stages as being essentially *egocentric* and unable to appreciate another person's point of view. Using more ecological and naturalistic methods researchers have found that children can, in fact, demonstrate many of these skills earlier than Piaget described, but there are no doubt significant changes in cognitive skills during school years (Donaldson, 1978).

Very young children, while obviously not receiving full-time formal education, can be nourished and encouraged in terms of their general abilities in many simple but important ways. The development of cognitive skills does not occur in isolation:

they can be stimulated within social interaction. If an adult has a good understanding of the child's ability, he or she can pitch interesting activities at a slightly more challenging level and so encourage development in a process described by Vygotsky (1962) as 'scaffolding'.

Play is often described as young children's work and every initiative taken to promote the ability and capacity of very young children to explore their environment in a playful way is likely to build their later resilience as it sets the foundations for cognitive development. Fantasy play usually begins to emerge at about 12–15 months. Pretend play tends to progress from actions like pretending to drink from an empty cup towards, by about 2 years, actions like making a doll drink from an empty cup. At the same time children increasingly use objects to represent other objects, for example, by 3 years children will spontaneously use bricks to represent cakes.

From a very young age children will also play with language, both when alone and with others. Between the ages of 3 and 6 pretend actions are put together so that everyday activities such as shopping or cooking are acted out, with children taking definite roles and using objects to represent other objects (Smith and Cowie 1991).

Adults can encourage such pretend activities. Even very young children are agents in their own development and it is often the way that their initiatives are met and responded to, as much as what is offered to the child, which can either promote or interrupt healthy assertion or exploration.

Any attempt to encourage children's natural curiosity is valuable in helping them to notice and attend to their environment, a prelude to the actual exploration. Carers can, and do, naturally model different forms of play so as to feed the creativity of the young child's imagination. Play can also be a release of tension, distraction from trouble and is therefore a potential comfort and resource to children, through which they can learn how to take basic care of themselves. Capacity to enjoy oneself in exploration is the foundation of a successful learning and offers multiple opportunities also for mastery.

Some children, however, who have had abusive or neglectful experiences may be reluctant to take any steps to explore their environment and need a great deal of gentle encouragement. Other children have never had the opportunity to play with others and need more adult support than one might imagine at their age. It is the *stage* of development that is the necessary focus of assessment from which the most fruitful strategies can then be based.

It may be worth remembering that many distressed children are somewhat physically passive and so deliberate active techniques involving movement, for example some form of physical exercise, can help the child to take a different perspective as it may well impact on the way the child feels.

When assessing who has the potential to offer early educational support, parents and other family members can be considered, even if children do not live with them. The most important issue is the need for someone to have detailed day-to-day knowledge of and interest in the child's development. Such a person could be a volunteer, mentor from the community, family member, play worker, nursery keyworker or the like.

✓

EDUCATION CHECKLIST
CHILD

The health visitor will be carrying out regular assessments of the child's development. Ensure that the health visitor is involved in the process of evaluating potential strengths or deficits in this domain.

Observe the child at home, in interaction with you and, if possible, with other children.

To what extent does the child show curiosity about his or her environment?

1. Does this child seem interested in his or her environment?

2. Can this child explore with confidence?

3. What does this child enjoy?

4. Does he or she show an interest in books?

5. Can this child concentrate on a play activity, for how long and is there potential to extend this?

6. Observe him or her playing. Are there any particular themes or preoccupations evident, and is there evidence of age-appropriate pretend play?

7. What opportunity does he or she have for solitary play which can be comforting and reassuring to him or her and which happens at his or her own pace?

To what extent does the parent or carer environment facilitate the child's cognitive development?

1. What opportunity does he or she have for imaginative play with adults?

2. What help from a trusted adult does he or she need to concentrate on activities and sustain play?

3. How does he or she respond to offers of help with an activity?

4.   What goals does the parent or carer seem to have for this child, for example, do they seem to have a view about what he or she needs to learn next?

5.   What might be it be helpful for a parent or carer to do now to promote healthy play and exploration?

6.   Can this child play cooperatively with adults?

7.   Does anyone read to and with the child?

What wider opportunities does this child have for cognitive stimulation?

1.   What opportunity does he or she have for shared play with at least one other child, even for brief periods?

2.   Does he or she have some access to a sufficient variety of toys, including some educational toys such as puzzles, shape games, books and so on?

3.   Is there a local toy library, and does the local library have a good children's section?

4.   Does he or she have a chance to take part in role play, drama or musical activities?

5.   Are there any other adults or older children (such as siblings) in the child's life who might be able to offer time to the child for play, reading, learning support and so on?

6.   Are there any local play groups, toddlers' groups or clubs for small children that he or she attends or might benefit from attending?

EDUCATION CHECKLIST
PARENT/CARER

If the child is attending any pre-school provision involve staff in the assessment.

To what extent does the child show curiosity about his or her environment?

Ask the parent/carer:

1. Does your child seem interested in his or her environment?

2. Do you find that he or she will explore new places and toys with confidence?

3. What does this child enjoy?

4. Does he or she show interest in books?

5. Do you find that he or she can concentrate on a play activity for a reasonable time?

6. Do you see any particular themes in his or her play, for example, does he or she play pretend shopping, cooking, houses and so on?

7. Do you find that you can leave him or her to play alone for some periods of the day?

To what extent does the parent or carer environment facilitate the child's cognitive development?

Ask the parent/carer:

1. Do you find that you can play imaginative games with him or her, or is this something that you would welcome some advice on?

2. Have you found any ways of encouraging him or her to concentrate for longer on play and activities?

3. How does he or she react if you offer to play with him or her (for example, with pleasure or in a rejecting way)?

4. What do you think it is important for your child to learn next?

5. What would you like to be able to do to help him or her with play and development?

6. Do you think he or she can play cooperatively with adults?

7. Do you have time to read with your child? Would you find it helpful to have some advice about good books for little children?

What wider opportunities does this child have for cognitive stimulation?

Ask the parent/carer:

1. Are there other children in the neighbourhood that he or she can play with? Is this something that is easy for you to arrange?

2. Do you think that you have enough educational toys such as puzzles, shape games, books and so on, or would you like help with this?

3. Do you know if there is a local toy library, and does the local library have a good children's section? Would you like help with finding and using such facilities?

4. Does he or she have a chance to take part in role play, drama or musical activities? If not, what sort of thing do you think he or she would most enjoy?

5. Can you think of anyone else in the family or among friends who might have the time and interest to offer time to the child for play, reading, learning support and so on?

6. Are there any local play groups, toddlers' groups or clubs for small children that he or she attends? Would you like some help finding out about what might be on offer locally?

5
Friendships

Background information

> From a remarkably early age, children not only can describe their various network associates, but can offer candid appraisals of the extent of support they expect from each. (Thompson 1995, p.34)

Resilience is associated with having generally positive peer relationships, and, specifically, good friendships (Werner, 1990). Much research has been carried out about the importance of social support for adults and more is emerging about the importance of such social support for children. It is known that having friends can help buffer the effects of stress, prevent stress, mediate stress and provide information to deal with stress. The key issue for adults appears to be the perception of having support (Thompson, 1995). The issues for children are similar, but there are unique features of their friendships due to developmental stage, autonomy and power. Friendships in childhood allow for horizontal (equal) relationships, which complement the vertical relationships they have with adults. This allows them to learn the social skills of interacting with equals, such as competition and cooperation and in this way children socialise each other (Schaffer 1996). Friends are also for fun and companionship: children enjoy activities much more if they are carried out with friends rather than non-friends (Foot, Morgan and Shute 1990, cited in Schaffer 1996). Hartup (1992) describes friendships as also providing:

- contexts in which to acquire or elaborate social skills
- self-knowledge and knowledge about others

- emotional support in times of stress
- the basis for future intimate relationships.

Conversely, the lack of friends during childhood is associated with a range of problems (Schaffer 1996):

- emotional problems
- immature perspective-taking ability
- less altruism
- poor social skills in group entry, cooperative play and conflict management
- less sociability
- poor school adjustment
- poorer school attainment.

There is likely to be a circular pattern whereby children who already show problems such as aggressiveness and poor social skills have difficulty in making friends and are therefore less likely to have the opportunity to learn better skills. It is a matter of concern if a young child appears to have generally poor peer relationships because the quality of early experiences of peer relationships provides the basis for the development of more specific friendships in later years.

From a young age children need relationships with adults and with other children, so that they can develop a network of attachments (Holmes 1993). Although good peer relationships can compensate to some extent for poor attachment experiences, there is evidence of an association between the quality of attachments and the quality of friendships. Children with secure attachments tend to relate to peers in a positive and responsive way, whereas children with insecure avoidant attachments may show either aggression towards or detachment from peers (Howe 1995). Social support can buffer the effects of adversity, but maltreatment can impair peer relationships so that those who need social support the most are the least likely to have it (Thompson 1995). Therefore, children with insecure attachments to parents or carers, or who have been abused or neglected may need extra help with peer relationships.

From a very young age infants are interested in their peers, although the interest will be mainly demonstrated by looking. They may engage in very short interactions of smiling, making sounds or showing toys. Between 2 and 4 there is a great increase in social skills with peers. During this time children will start to modify their play according to whom they are playing with, in other words, they take more account of other children as individuals (Schaffer 1996). When with peers pre-schoolers divide their time between solitary play (playing alone), parallel play (playing near each other with the same toys, but without much interaction) and group play (small groups of two or three children engaged in joint activity). The level of parallel play stays fairly constant, but group play gradually increases, and this continues into school years (Smith and Cowie 1991). As verbal skills and the capacity for symbolic play increase, so the games of young children become more complex (Schaffer 1996).

Specific friendships are less marked in younger than older children. Younger children will play rather indiscriminately with other children in the neighbourhood and friendship is normally based upon proximity (Smith and Cowie 1991). Young children themselves describe friends in terms of proximity or as the people they play with (Bigelow and La Gaipa 1980). However, by 2 some children already show a preference for a specific playmate in nursery settings, and by 4 many will have one 'strong associate' (Hinde et al. 1985).

Young children's social networks are mainly centred around home and family, although the use of day care can widen networks (Thompson 1995). Of course, younger children's access to peers and potential friends is very dependent upon adults: it is mainly parents and carers who influence the nature and extent of children's peer networks. Younger children's play with other children is also frequently in the presence of adults, who can intervene as problems occur. The willingness of adults to supervise and intervene appropriately can therefore affect children's social skills development.

FRIENDSHIPS CHECKLIST
CHILD

With very young children much of the assessment will depend upon the reports of others and direct observation. However, with older children it should be possible to use dolls, drawing and games to gauge their emerging readiness for friendship.

What characteristics does this child have that help with making and keeping friends?

1. Before carrying out direct assessment with the child it would be helpful to know the names of children he or she knows and, if possible, some photos.

2. Use your direct contact with the child and observations of him or her with others to assess whether the child seems very shy with others, very aggressive towards others, or appropriate in approach.

3. Use dolls, drawings, toys and/or photos of other known children to explore who the child might call a friend. For example, one doll can be used to represent this child playing a game. Another doll can be brought into the game and the child asked 'And who is this one going to be?' and so on.

4. Use similar materials to explore what the child's understanding of friendships is. For example, the dolls can be 'playing' and the child asked to show what happens when the dolls are playing.

5. With some older children it will be possible to ask them who their friends are, and what friends are.

✓

To what extent does the parent or carer environment facilitate the development of friendship?

1. Does the parent or carer recognise that even very young children need time to play with other children?

2. What opportunities are there for the parent or carer to encourage play, for example, do any of their friends or family have young children?

3. Does the parent go to any parent and toddler groups?

4. Does the parent supervise any of the child's play and intervene appropriately to encourage friendly interactions?

5. Is there any indication that the child has an insecure attachment pattern that is hampering friendship, for example is he or she excessively 'clingy' to the parent, or very detached from other children?

What are the child's friendships like at the moment?

1. If at all possible arrange to observe this child playing with other children and see what proportions of time are spent in solitary, parallel and group play.

2. Does the child appear to have any preference for a particular child? By 4 children could have what has been called a 'strong associate'; is this the case here?

3. With very young children you need to observe their reactions to other children. Do they show interest in them, perhaps reaching out, handing things or touching them?

**FRIENDSHIPS CHECKLIST
PARENT/CARER**

What characteristics does this child have that help with making and keeping friends?

Ask the parent/carer:

1. How does this child get on with other children? Does he or she seem a lot shyer than other children, or a lot more pushy, or does he or she play well with others?

2. Does your child play with any other children that you might call their 'friends' (taking account of the developmental stage)?

3. Do you think he or she is developing an idea of what friends are and why children like to have friends?

To what extent does the parent or carer environment facilitate the development of friendship?

Ask the parent/carer:

1. What do you think your child gets from spending time with other children?

2. How easy is it for you to help your child spend time with other children? For example, do you have any friends or family who also have young children?

3. Are there any parent–toddler groups in your area that you can or do attend? If there isn't one, would you like there to be?

4. Do you get much chance to see how your child plays with other children? How do you normally help your child to play nicely with other children?

5. Are you ever worried that your child seems too clingy, or is not interested in other children?

What are the child's friendships like at the moment?

Take some time to describe solitary, parallel and group play to the parent and then ask: 'Tell me about the way your child plays with other children, how much time do you think he or she spends in each of these different kinds of play?'
Ask the parent/carer:

1. Does your child appear to get on especially well with any other child? Do you think your child has what might be called a 'best friend'?

2. (For very young children) Have you noticed how your baby reacts to other babies and children? Does he or she show an interest in them by looking, reaching out, touching and so on?

The Early Years, © Brigid Daniel and Sally Wassell 2002 © Iain Campbell 2002

6

Talents and Interests

Background information

Self-esteem is one of the fundamental building blocks of resilience. Self-esteem has been defined as: 'Appreciating my own worth and importance and having the character to be accountable for myself and to act responsibly toward others' (California State Department of Education, cited in Brooks 1994, p.547).

This definition highlights the importance of the interpersonal element of self-esteem. Having a healthy sense of self-esteem is not just about feeling good about oneself while having no regard for the impact of oneself upon others. Therefore, the goal of much long-term work with children is not only to help them to feel better about themselves, but also to help them recognise the importance of interrelationships and of empathy with others. Self-esteem appears to be linked with levels of self-efficacy which is also known to be associated with resilience and which is discussed in more detail in the Social Competence domain (Luthar, 1991). So, children with high self-esteem have a realistic notion of their abilities and see successes as due to their own efforts and within their control. Those with low esteem are more likely to attribute any successes to chance. They see failures as due to un-changeable factors, for example a lack of ability or intelligence. They demonstrate a sense of helplessness and hopelessness, expect to fail and show self-defeating behaviour (Brooks 1994).

Harter (1985) suggests that self-esteem is based in the balance between what children would like to be and what they think they actually are. Everyone has an 'ideal' self and a 'perceived' self, and the closer they are to each other, the healthier the self-esteem (Schaffer and Emerson 1964). Self-esteem is not simply related to being good at something. A child may be very good at drawing, but not value that skill. Also, a child who would like to be good at drawing, but perceives that his or her drawings are poor, will have a lower esteem than a child who does not value art and whose drawings are poor.

In her studies of self-esteem, Harter (1985) looked at a global measure of self-esteem (general self-worth) as well as five separate domains:

- scholastic competence
- athletic competence
- social acceptance
- physical appearance
- behavioural conduct.

Harter found the different domains to be independent of each other, so for example, a child might have a high score in one area and a low one in another. It is not until children reach the age of about 6 or 7 that a reliable, separate global rating of self-esteem can be measured. So, younger children's self-esteem can fluctuate and vary according to circumstances (Harter 1985). Self-esteem can change and is amenable to improvement.

The roots of esteem lie firmly in early attachment experiences and enduring feelings based on early experiences of being loved. During the early years sensitive, warm and accepting parenting in the context of at least one secure attachment is fundamental to the development of good self-esteem.

Therefore, encouraging the child's unique talents and interests can help to boost resilience. If a child has a natural talent it should be nurtured, and, more importantly, the child should learn to value that talent. If a child has an interest, that interest should be supported, even if the child has no special talent in the area. Many children who have experienced adversity and who may be either at home or 'looked after' may have hidden attributes and potential that have not emerged under conditions of stress and confusion. For example, the child who is preoccupied with surviving abuse, or living with domestic violence, may have learned to use his or her energies in adapting to complex or changing family circumstances, and hence will not have had the chance or energy to make use of available opportunities. Those children who adapt to stress and trauma by becoming passive or those with particularly low self-esteem, may have little or no sense of their own particular aptitudes. The challenge for practitioners is therefore to find ways of creating opportunities for young people to experience feelings of success, perhaps by looking for 'islands of competence' (Brooks 1994).

Remarkably, some children still demonstrate unusual capacities and abilities, even in the most stressful circumstances and here the continuity of opportunity through any necessary changes or transitions will be of real importance. For example, the child who shows skill in physical coordination, who has enjoyed gymnastics and yet has to leave home or move to another placement, will benefit from continuing with the activity if at all possible.

✓

**TALENTS AND INTERESTS CHECKLIST
CHILD**

What talents does this child have and does he or she have any particular interests?

Remember that what the child is interested in and what he or she is good at might be different. The older children in this age group might also be developing views about what skills they place value on.

1. Along with the child draw a range of activities, or use catalogues and magazines to cut out pictures of activities (footballs, cycles, swimming, tennis racquets etc.) and use this game as a way to trigger discussion with the child about activities that might interest him or her.

2. One of the best ways to gauge the skills and interests of a young child is to take part in them with the child, involving the parent wherever possible. Try out a range of activities for example:

    (a) Go to a local sports centre and try out different activities with the child; try to interest a member of staff in helping you find out whether the child shows aptitude in, for example, hand–eye coordination.

    (b) Take the child to a pre-school gymnastics club.

    (c) Locate a music teacher (or perhaps music therapist) who would be prepared to make some music with the child and assess his or her interest and/or ability.

    (d) Take the child to a pre-school drama or dance club.

    (e) Spend time drawing, painting and modelling with the child.

    (f) Play construction games or make models with the child.

3. Ask all the people who the child spends time with (especially nursery key staff) whether they have noticed him or her to show any particular interests or skills.

Does the parent or carer environment encourage the development and expression of talents and interests?

From discussions with all involved (including the child where possible), and your observations, form a view about the following areas:

1. Does anyone in the family appear to be interested in the same things as the child?

2. Does anyone in the family have a hobby that a young child could be involved in to an extent?

3. Are the parents or carers able to help the child to develop interests, and if not what would help?

4. How interested do you think that the parent or carer is in the child's developing talents and interests?

What opportunities are there in the wider environment for the nurturing of this child's talents and interests?

1. Does there seem to be anyone in the extended family who might help the child to develop an interest (for example, grandparent, older sibling, uncle or aunt, friend's parent and so on)?

2. What local hobby clubs or groups exist in the area local to the child? Consider first the mainstream community activities before looking at special projects.

3. Explore what kinds of activities are on offer at local nurseries and toddlers' groups, for example, some specialise in outdoor activities. Are there any that place special emphasis on developing children's individual talents and interests?

4. Is there scope for the involvement of a mentor, keyworker or volunteer to help develop the child's talents and interests?

✓

TALENTS AND INTERESTS CHECKLIST
PARENT/CARER

What talents does this child have and does he or she have any particular interests?

Explain to the parent or carer that what the child is interested in and what he or she is good at might be different and that the older ones might be starting to develop views about what skills they would value.

Ask the parent/carer:

1. What activities and other things has your child shown an interest in?

2. Can you think of any activities that your child seems to enjoy, for example, dressing up, drawing, make-believe, outdoor games, sports?

3. Does your child show signs of having a particular skill or talent, for example, in painting, throwing and catching and so on? If so, does he or she enjoy being good at that skill?

4. (For the older children) Do you know what activities and skills that your child is starting to see as important to be good at?

5. Do you think there are any other activities that your child might enjoy trying?

Does the parent or carer environment encourage the development and expression of talents and interests?

Ask the parent/carer:

1. Are there activities that you enjoy, do you have time to take part in them, and could they be shared with your child?

2. Does anyone in your family have a hobby that your child does, or could share?

3. Do you find that you are able to help your child take part in activities? If not, what gets in the way, for example, lack of time, money or energy?

What opportunities are there in the wider environment for the nurturing of this child's talents and interests?

Ask the parent/carer:

1. Can you think of anyone you know who might help your child do something he or she is interested in (for example, grandparent, older sibling, uncle or aunt, friends and so on)?

2. Do you know of local pre-school clubs or groups near where you live that your child does, or would like to attend? If not, would you like help finding out this information?

3. Do you know of any nurseries or toddlers' groups near where you live that offer a good range of activities. Would you like more information about this?

4. Is there anyone else that you think could help your child to develop a talent or interest, for example, neighbour, volunteer or keyworker?

7

Positive Values

Background information

Holding positive values and having the capacity to act in a helpful, caring and responsible way towards others is associated with resilience (Benson 1997; Raundalen 1991; Werner and Smith 1992). Such 'prosocial' behaviour is displayed in actions towards others that are not based on the expectation of external rewards (Smith and Cowie 1991) and include:

- helping others

- comforting others in distress

- sharing with others.

Prosocial behaviour depends on the stage of cognitive and emotional development and on the development of empathy. That is, the child must have an understanding that other people have feelings, must have empathy for those feelings, have the ability to act kindly towards others and be able to inhibit negative actions.

Young children cannot fully understand about morality, nor can they be expected to have a mature conscience. Young children do not have the cognitive capacity to engage in sophisticated moral reasoning and tend to operate at what has been described as a 'preconventional' moral reasoning level (Kohlberg 1969). (See Appendix for more information about stages of moral reasoning.) From about the age of 4 they begin to develop moral reasoning, but until about 9 or 10 they tend to judge the morality of an action by the outcome rather than the intent, for example, to break ten cups accidentally is seen as worse than to break one deliberately. During the early years it is parents and other caretakers who must provide boundaries and act as the child's 'external conscience', providing explanations as they intervene.

By 9 to 12 months infants begin to recognise different emotions in others (Smith and Cowie 1991). By 2 years of age they spontaneously use a range of emotion words, such as 'scared' and 'fun', and by 28 months use language to comment on their own and others' feelings. By the age of 4 most children can demonstrate that they have developed what has been called a 'theory of mind', that is the ability to work out what other people are thinking and feeling. By the age of 5 they can describe situations that will generate feelings of happiness, sadness, anger, fear and shyness, in other words, emotions that tend to be shown in facial expressions (Harris *et al.* 1987; Terwogt and Stegge 1998).

Pre-school children will normally demonstrate prosocial behaviour by acting on their understanding about others' feelings. Before the age of about 20 months children may become upset when they observe another's distress, for example crying when another child cries. After about 20 months children begin to develop an understanding of cause and effect and have a clearer sense of the separation between self and other. From this age children are more likely to try to comfort, help or reassure someone in distress. Young children will spontaneously try to help adults with chores. Some observations also suggest that 10–20 per cent of nursery children's social interactions are prosocial (Bar-Tal, Raviv and Goldberg 1982).

There are several aspects of care-giving that are known to encourage the development of prosocial behaviour. Warm and secure attachment to a caregiver provides the basis for the development of empathy and for the understanding that others have feelings that can be influenced. If the attachment figure models kind behaviour then this is highly influential because children imitate people they identify with. Young children also respond to clear rules and expectations of behaviour towards others. Parents with children who show prosocial behaviour tend to (Schaffer 1996; Zahn-Waxler, Radke-Yarrow and King 1979):

- provide clear rules and principles for behaviour, reward kindness, show disapproval of unkindness and explain the effects of hurting others

- present moral messages in an emotional rather than calm manner

- attribute prosocial qualities to the child by telling him or her frequently that they are kind and helpful

- model prosocial behaviour themselves
- provide empathic care-giving to the child.

In summary the modelling of prosocial behaviour by significant adults is highly influential and the parent or carer is more effective if their messages about prosocial behaviour contain an emotional element, that is messages about behaviour should not necessarily be given in a cool and detached way. Children need to see that prosocial behaviour is to do with emotions and feelings, specifically the feelings of others.

The indicator for mapping this area is the child's behaviour towards others. This can be assessed by direct observation, discussions with parents, nursery staff, keyworkers and carers and conversations with the child. It should be possible to check the child's ability to take the perspective of others by, for example, using stories or play figures to create situations where something good or bad happens and exploring what the child thinks the subjects may have felt.

Attention to the young person's capacity for empathy is crucial. Such empathy need be demonstrated not only towards people; children who are cruel to animals may well go on to behave cruelly to other children.

If a young child is already demonstrating positive actions towards others then this is very hopeful. It indicates a level of empathy, which in turn can be linked with self-esteem and an understanding that other people have feelings. Therefore, prosocial behaviour should be reinforced wherever possible and intervention to boost resilience can be built upon existing positive values, for example, by involving young children in helping with household tasks.

If a young child is not demonstrating positive values, then this should be considered a priority area for targeted intervention to boost resilience. The younger such behaviour can be encouraged the better, especially as there appears to be continuity between how kind a child is when young and when older (Dunn and Kendrick 1982). The ecological model is highly important here because the social environment exerts such a strong influence over children's social behaviour. Situations need to be created that require young people to care for and be responsible towards others. Raundalen (1991), for example, suggests that children's empathic behaviour can be enhanced through encouraging interest in the environment and nature and by giving opportunities for caring for pets.

Foster parents, nursery staff and other professionals in a caring role need to be able to put over the emotional messages when giving challenging messages about antisocial, unkind or cruel behaviour towards others. Although the professional role often requires calmness, and acceptance, this has to be balanced with the 'human' elements of an adult–child relationship that foster empathy and positive values.

✓ POSITIVE VALUES CHECKLIST
CHILD

With younger children a mixture of techniques will be required to assess the following areas including observation and direct interaction using drawings, photos of people showing different emotions, cards depicting facial expressions, play figures, cartoon scenarios and so on.

To what extent can this child take the perspective of others?

1. Use the pictures 'Emotional faces' that follow or photos depicting different emotions to explore the child's recognition and understanding of emotions. For example, the young child can be asked to point to the happy face, sad face etc. The child can also be asked to act out the feelings of the faces. Describe a scenario, for example, that of a child falling over and ask which face would show the reaction?

2. Assess whether the child has the language to convey his or her own feelings.

3. Try a simple version of the kind of tasks used to explore whether children have a 'theory of mind'.

4. Use the pictures 'Emotional scenes' that follow to explore what feelings the child thinks that the characters will experience in different situations.

To what extent does this child engage in helping behaviour?

1. Observe the child during part of a normal day with a parent, carer or other significant adult.

2. Does he or she show any spontaneous attempts to help with household tasks?

3. What is his or her response when asked to help?

4. How does the adult encourage helping, for example, do they praise, encourage, punish or ignore?

Do what extent does this child show comforting or sharing behaviour?

Observe the child during play with other children, either at home or in a nursery setting.

1. When another child is upset, either because of the actions of this child or other children, or because of an accident, does this child show any actions that appear to be aimed at comforting, for example, patting, kissing, hugging, getting help?

2. How often does the child spontaneously share toys or activities with other children?

3. How does the child react if another child wants to share a toy or activity with them?

EMOTIONAL FACES

The Early Years, © Brigid Daniel and Sally Wassell 2002 © Iain Campbell 2002

Emotional faces legends

Happy

Sad

Frightened

Angry

THEORY OF MIND

Psychological experiments have been carried out to test at what age children develop a theory of mind. Here, two of such tasks that could be adapted for use in practice are summarised (Lewis and Osborne 1990; Perner, Leekam and Wimmer 1987; Smith and Cowie 1991).

1. Before meeting with the child obtain a Smartie box and place a pencil in it, put the lid on. Show the child the Smartie box and ask them what they think is inside. Most young children will think it is Smarties. Then take off the lid and show them that it is only a pencil. Put the lid on and check they remember what is in the box. Then ask the following question that tests whether they know that they had a false belief:

   'What did you think was in the box before I took the top off?'

   and one that tests whether they know that others can hold a false belief:

   'What will [name of friend] think is in the box before I take the top off?'

   Most 3-year-olds can do this correctly.

2. This is a more action-oriented version of the above (Freeman, Lewis and Doherty 1991), which some young children perform better on, but as it involves a hide-and-seek scenario, it should not be used for children for whom hiding is associated with abuse.

   Using small cardboard boxes make a simple set-up that represents two sheds, one red and one yellow. They each have doors and a small door inside between them. Draw a pathway to each in the same colour. Use two play figures to represent a child and an adult (give them appropriate names) who are playing hide-and-seek. The child runs down the yellow path to hide while the adult counts to ten, but the adult cheats by peeping and sees the child going into the yellow shed. Once in the shed the child crawls through the little joining door into the red shed. You can then ask the question that tests for the false belief:

   'Where do you think the adult will look for the child?'

   and the question that tests for reality:

   'Where is the child?'

EMOTIONAL SCENES

The Early Years, © Brigid Daniel and Sally Wassell 2002 © Iain Campbell 2002

Emotional scenes legends

Frightened

Happy

Angry

Sad

✔

POSITIVE VALUES CHECKLIST
PARENT/CARER

To what extent can this child take the perspective of others?

Ask the parent/carer:

1.   What emotions does this child appear to recognise in others?

2.   What emotions does this child appear to recognise in him or herself?

3.   What emotion words does this child have and are they used appropriately?

4.   To what extent do you think this child can put him or herself in another's place?

To what extent does this child engage in helping behaviour?

Ask the parent/carer:

1.   How often does the child spontaneously try to help you with household chores?

2.   How does he or she usually respond if you ask for help?

3.   How would you normally encourage him or her to help? Do you prompt the child to help, praise the child when he or she does, punish the child if he or she won't, or do you not expect the child to help yet?

To what extent does this child show comforting or sharing behaviour?

Ask the parent/carer:

1. When this child is playing with other children how does your child react if another child is distressed, either because of his or her own or another child's actions or an accident? Have you seen your child try to comfort others?

2. Have you seen the child spontaneously share toys or activities with other children?

3. How does your child usually react if another child wants to share a toy or activity with him or her?

8

Social Competencies

Background information

The capacity for social competence has been demonstrated to be associated with resilience (Luther 1991; Werner and Smith 1992). It is very difficult to pin down 'social competence' because it covers such a wide range of skills and attributes, many of them very closely intertwined with those associated with the Positive Values and Friendships domains. A useful definition is that developed by a Scottish Executive funded initiative, the Promoting Social Competence project based at Dundee University (Promoting Social Competence 1999):

> Social Competence is possessing and using the ability to integrate thinking, feeling and behaviour to achieve social tasks and outcomes valued in the host context and culture.

The definition goes on to incorporate:

> perception of relevant social cues, interpretation of social cues, realistic anticipation of obstacles to personally desired behaviour, anticipation of consequences of behaviour for self and others, generation of effective solutions to interpersonal problems, translation of social decisions into effective social behaviours, and the expression of a positive sense of self-efficacy.

Bernard (1991) identifies a group of factors that indicate resilience:

- social competence
- autonomy, also known as internal locus of control
- capacity for problem-solving
- sense of purpose and future.

The foundations for social competence are laid in early childhood. The development of autonomy has been described as one of the key developmental tasks for a toddler (Erikson 1963). Autonomy describes the ability to operate as an independent individual and underpins social competence. With the development of appropriate autonomy the child increasingly learns how to master the social and physical world and develops a sense of self-efficacy.

The development of self-efficacy depends in part upon the development of accurate explanations for events and the behaviour of oneself and others. These 'attributions', as they are known, have three components (Peterson and Seligman 1985). The first is whether the cause for an event is attributed to internal characteristics of the person, or to external, situational factors. For example, a young child asks a neighbouring child to come and play in her garden and the child refuses. The child could make an internal attribution 'She doesn't like me' or an external attribution 'Her mum has told her to stay in her own garden'. The second component is whether the cause is seen as stable over time or transient. For example 'She'll never be my friend' or 'Maybe when she knows me better she'll be my friend'. The third component concerns whether the cause is seen to apply globally or specifically, 'No one will be my friend' or 'It is only this girl that won't be my friend'. As they mature children need to develop reasonably accurate attributions about their own and others' behaviour. Young children who have suffered abuse or severe loss often develop attributions that are internal, stable and global: 'It's my fault, it's going to last forever and it will affect everything I do'.

Very young children enjoy the feeling of mastery they gain from having an impact upon the physical or social environment. At a young age children can begin to assess the extent and limits of their own ability, and a 2-year-old, for example, is upset when an adult models a task that the child cannot do (Masten and Coatsworth 1998). As well as autonomy and self-efficacy, young children begin to develop skills that help them with self-control. They develop the skills of self-regulation that include control of attention, of emotions and of their behaviour (Masten and Coatsworth 1998). During early years children become better at directing their attention, focusing their attention and persisting in attendance on tasks. The lack of ability to regulate attention has been associated with a range of problems with social competence (Masten and Coatsworth 1998). Clearly young children need to develop skills in paying attention to social cues. The ability to cope with stress and anxiety is also associated with social competence, and children with a 'difficult' temperament in early childhood can develop aggressive and disruptive behaviour later.

The early signs of self-control emerge in the second year and it is around then that parents will normally begin to communicate rules and expectations of behaviour (Masten and Coatsworth 1998). Thus there is a process of socialisation of the child to the rules of the immediate family, and increasingly to the rules of the wider society. Self-control without constant adult supervision is normally shown in the third year. Children will, in fact, also be learning an important distinction between rules of social conventions and universal rules of morality. As their prosocial skills develop so they will begin to appreciate the importance of moral rules against harm to others for example (see Positive Values domain). Even young children can make the distinction between social convention and universal rules (Schaffer 1996).

Social skills are usually learnt initially within the context of attachment relationships and are then extended to peers and other adults. In order to develop appropriate social skills young children require an authoritative parental environment where warmth and sensitivity are coupled with the provision of clear boundaries and requirements for behaviour. The toddler's urge for autonomy has to be respected within appropriate and safe limits, for example, by allowing the child to choose between two options for clothing, or between two different places for an outing. Finally, young children need the opportunity to play with other children so that they can learn how to read social situations and how to become integrated into them.

Children who have been deprived of secure early attachment relationships are likely to require considerable support in the development of social skills. Young children may show aggressive behaviour, when they do not have the language to express what they want they may grab and hit. However, such instrumental aggression (aimed at getting something you want) normally declines between the ages of 4 and 7. Individual differences in aggression level are apparent at very young ages and the differences persist over many years (Schaffer 1996). There can be a damaging interaction between a child with a temperamental tendency towards violence and parents under stress who also routinely use aggression and violence. The fact that aggression persists over time indicates the need for early intervention in such situations.

SOCIAL COMPETENCIES CHECKLIST
CHILD

As described in the introduction, the term 'social competence' covers a wide range of cognitive, affective and behavioural factors. The focus here will primarily be upon cognitive and behavioural aspects of social competence because the affective aspects are essentially assessed in the Positive Values domain. Peer relationships are obviously a crucial indicator of social competence and although touched on here are assessed in detail in the Friendships domain.

To what extent do this child's personal characteristics contribute to his or her level of social competence?

1. Observe the child's interactions with significant others, including parents and carers, siblings and, where appropriate, yourself.

2. Use the provided Social Attributes Checklist (McClellan and Katz 1992) to assess the social competency of the child.

Assess the child on the following aspects of social competence.

AUTONOMY

Does the child assert his or her own personality, does he or she ask why they have to do certain things, does he or she try to do things for him or herself, can the child separate from the carer in a healthy way?

SELF-CONTROL

Does the child exert some measure of control over his or her behaviour, at a level that can normally be expected of a toddler, does he or she show excessive levels of aggression?

TEMPERAMENT

Is the child normally cheerful, does he or she demonstrate a sense of humour, can he or she be comforted after a set-back, does he or she respond openly to overtures from adults?

SELF-EFFICACY

Does the child make attempts to try out new tasks, does he or she appear to have a rudimentary understanding of the limits of his or her abilities?

ATTENTION

Can the child concentrate for periods of time on a particular task, can he or she be encouraged to listen to a story or to watch a short child's video, will he or she make a number of attempts to complete a difficult task?

To what extent does the parent or carer environment encourage social competencies?

Again, observe the child at home and assess the following:

1. Are there basic rules for social behaviour with which the child is encouraged and expected to comply, for example, saying 'please' and 'thank you', responding when greeted or asked a question, learning not to interrupt others, looking at people when they address him or her, turn-taking in conversation and games, asking for things he or she wants rather than grabbing them?

2. Is the parental environment 'authoritative'? In other words, is it warm, but with appropriate boundaries for behaviour that are applied reasonably consistently?

What opportunities does this child have to develop competence in a wider social environment?

1. Does this child have the opportunity to play with other children of about his or her own age?

2. Is his or her play with other children sometimes supervised by an adult who appropriately intervenes and encourages give and take, sharing, turn-taking?

3. How well does the child respond to other adults, is he or she very shy, or overly friendly?

✓

SOCIAL ATTRIBUTES CHECKLIST

This checklist (McClellan and Katz 1992) is available on the internet from the ERIC Digest at http://www.ed.gov/databases/ERIC_Digests/index/. Items on the digest are for public use and there is a range of articles relating to resilience that may be of use.

Individual attributes

The child:

1. Is USUALLY in a positive mood

2. Is not EXCESSIVELY dependent on the teacher, assistant or other adults

3. USUALLY comes to the program or setting willingly

4. USUALLY copes with rebuffs and reverses adequately

5. Shows the capacity to empathise

6. Has positive relationship with one or two peers; shows capacity to really care about them, miss them if absent, etc.

7. Displays the capacity for humour

8. Does not seem to be acutely or chronically lonely.

Social skills attributes

The child USUALLY:

1. Approaches others positively

2. Expresses wishes and preferences clearly; gives reasons for actions and positions

3. Asserts own rights and needs appropriately

4. Is not easily intimidated by bullies

5. Expresses frustrations and anger effectively and without harming others or property

6. Gains access to ongoing groups at play and work

7. Enters ongoing discussion on the subject; makes relevant contributions to ongoing activities

8. Takes turns fairly easily

9. Shows interest in others; exchanges information with and requests information from others appropriately

10. Negotiates and compromises with others appropriately

11. Does not draw inappropriate attention to self

12. Accepts and enjoys peers and adults of ethnic groups other than his or her own

13. Interacts non-verbally with other children with smiles, waves, nods, etc.

Peer relationship attributes

The child is:

1. USUALLY accepted versus neglected or rejected by other children

2. SOMETIMES invited by other children to join them in play, friendship and work.

✓

SOCIAL COMPETENCIES CHECKLIST
PARENT/CARER

To what extent do this child's personal characteristics contribute to his or her level of social competence?

Ask the parent/carer about the following aspects of social competence.

AUTONOMY

Does the child assert his or her own personality, does he or she ask why they have to do certain things, does he or she try to do things for him or herself, can the child separate from you in a healthy way?

SELF-CONTROL

Does the child exert some measure of control over his or her behaviour at a level that can normally be expected of a toddler, does he or she show excessive levels of aggression?

TEMPERAMENT

Is the child normally cheerful, does she or he show a sense of humour, can he or she be comforted after a set-back, how does he or she respond to approaches from adults?

SELF-EFFICACY

Does the child make attempts to try out new things, does he or she appear to have a basic understanding of the limits of his or her abilities?

ATTENTION

Can the child concentrate for periods of time on a particular task, can he or she be encouraged to listen to a story, will he or she watch a short child's video, will he or she make a number of attempts to complete a difficult task?

To what extent does the parent or carer environment encourage social competencies?

Ask the parent/carer:

1. What aspects of social behaviour do you believe to be important and how do you encourage such behaviour (for example saying 'please' and 'thank you', responding when greeted or asked a question, learning not to interrupt others, looking at people when they address him or her, turn-taking in conversation and games, asking for things he or she wants rather than grabbing them)?

2. What is your approach to discipline (for example, can you find ways to deal with tantrums, can you predict situations that might cause problems, can you distract the child or offer alternatives to avoid confrontations)?

What opportunities does this child have to develop competence in a wider social environment?

Ask the parent/carer:

1. Does your child have the opportunity to play with other children of about his or her own age?

2. Is his or her play with other children sometimes supervised by an adult who appropriately intervenes and encourages give and take, sharing, turn-taking?

3. How well does your child respond to other adults, is he or she very shy or overly friendly, and so on?

Part II

Intervention

9
Intervention Strategies

Introduction

It is beyond the scope of these workbooks to give comprehensive intervention guidance. By its very nature, practice that aims to promote resilience has to be individually tailored to suit each individual child or young person and his or her unique circumstances. Instead, principles to underpin the planning of intervention are outlined and for each domain examples of possible intervention strategies are provided. Practitioners are encouraged to be as creative as possible in developing these strategies further to meet individual needs.

The balancing act

It can be difficult to decide whether to build upon existing strengths or whether to concentrate on boosting areas of less strength. Five strategies for intervention have been suggested (Masten 1994):

- reduce vulnerability and risk

- reduce the number of stressors and pile-up

- increase the available resources

- mobilise protective processes

- foster resilience strings (where an improvement in one domain has a positive knock-on effect in other domains).

We would recommend that practitioners strive to strike a balance between these different approaches. Current practice is frequently characterised by risk reduction and therefore more attention may need to be paid to looking for strengths and building upon them. Wherever possible a strength in one domain can be used to boost a weaker domain. For example, if a child has a strong attachment to a member of the extended family (Secure Base = strong), but takes part in no activities or hobbies (Talents and Interests = weak), the attachment figure can be encouraged and supported in helping the child to take part in an activity. Similarly, if a child has a good friend (Friendships = strong), but misses a lot of school (Education = weak), consideration could be given to involving the friend in encouragement to attend, perhaps by arranging for them to travel together.

The holistic approach

The resilient child can be described as one who can say (Grotsberg 1997):

> I HAVE
>
> I AM
>
> I CAN

For example, the child can say 'I have people who love me and people to help me', 'I am a likeable person and respectful of myself and others' and 'I can find ways to solve problems and can control myself'. The three categories loosely equate with the three building blocks of secure base, self-esteem and self-efficacy. The aim of intervention would be to develop all the domains so that the child can make such positive statements about him or herself:

> I HAVE: this could be boosted via work on Secure Base and Friendships
>
> I AM: this could be boosted via Positive Values and Social Competencies
>
> I CAN: this could be boosted via Education and Talents and Interests.

The ecological approach

As has been stressed throughout the workbook, consider interventions at each ecological level. The following practice suggestions are grouped, as far as possible, into each ecological level, although there may well be considerable overlap.

Multi-agency, network approach

Finally, it is essential that the social worker does not attempt to carry out work on all the domains alone.

Any professional involved with the child and family must be involved in any planning discussions about boosting resilience and there must agreement about priorities and how to address them. For example, a residential keyworker may take the main role in working on talents and interests, but the school should also be informed of what these talents and interests are so that they can reinforce them.

The whole of the child's network of family and friends should be assessed for potential to help with boosting resilience. For example, a grandparent may be able to offer time to help with homework, or a friend's parent may be able to include the child on outings if given some financial help.

PRACTICE SUGGESTIONS
SECURE BASE

This domain of resilience acts as a focus for deliberate strategies fundamental to basic care routines for the very young child. These often simple strategies, applied with persistence and consistency, can strengthen the child's feeling of basic security and belonging. They may be introduced as a way of improving existing attachment relationships, or to help with the development of new ones. Although it is important for the child to be attached to the main carer, this should not preclude attention to relationships with other important people in the child's life. The improvement of attachment relationships will be most likely to promote healthy developmental progress and recovery from the impact of adversities. It is important to examine:

- the existing sense of a secure base within the child, and

- existing strengths in the family setting which can be harnessed, but also

- existing strengths in the community and professional resources.

A useful paradigm, as described above, defines the resilient child as one who can make positive statements on each of three areas (Grotsberg 1997):

I HAVE

I AM

I CAN

These three perspectives link particularly directly with interventions around the provision of a secure base, that is, when building security and predictability for young children. Promoting a sense in children that they have relationships with significant people available to them and have a supportive environment is clearly relevant in the deliberate structuring of elements of the young child's environment in order to increase a sense of security. Such interventions mirror the functions of a secure or 'good enough' attachment relationship that acts to reduce anxiety and to promote healthy exploration and learning in the child at every stage of their development, but most particularly at the younger ages.

Every element of the young child's environment may act to reassure the child that he or she has available to them a net of security such as to communicate messages:

'I have reliable predictable adults available to me to offer support.'

'I have a reliable routine.'

The second helpful concept is the focus on the promotion of a sense of healthy identity as expressed in the phrase 'I am'. Attachment to a person who values the child for his or her intrinsic qualities will facilitate the development of good self-esteem, that is the ability to say 'I am a person worthy of love and attention'.

Care-givers need to make detailed attempts to structure the child's immediate care environment so as to make it possible for him or her to *achieve* in even a small way some aim which has salience for them. This may have particular importance, for example, for a child who has no sense of initiative and such a poorly developed sense of self-concept that he or she does not even know what they enjoy and are capable of. We know that a sense of achievement is an important component of self-esteem, and that this is facilitated by the messages of acceptance communicated by all the elements of a secure base.

Finally, it is possible to progress from the notion of 'I have' in relation to basic security, to 'I can' in relation to achievement. In other words, the child who has a basic sense of security, is more likely to feel that he or she can attempt new tasks and explore the environment in the search for mastery, and later incorporate these positive experiences into a confident self-identity. This requires the integration of experiences, opportunities, successes and problem-solving skills to the point where the child perceives these capacities and abilities as part of him or herself, not merely as a function of chance or a particular setting. In other words, the child develops a healthy sense of self-efficacy.

Helping the child to feel secure

1. Shape interventions deliberately in response to the child's attachment style, and remember that persistence will be required. For example, a child who avoids contact (avoidant attachment pattern) will need patiently available carers who do not press the child to come close but whose availability to offer support is nevertheless predictably present. A child who shows a combination of high levels of need for the carer combined with angry resistance (ambivalent attachment pattern) needs carers who have the patience and fortitude to withstand the demand and rejection: they need to help the child through the urge to reject closeness. A child whose responses are confused (disorganised attachment pattern) will need carers who can tolerate mixed responses and who are reliable and reassuring in their own responses. A child who shows clinging, anxious preoccupation with presence of the attachment figure (anxious attachment pattern) needs reassurance of carer responses that are as *predictable* as it is possible to provide, with only gradual encouragement in surviving brief separations.

2. Even very young children are capable of sharing jokes with adults and this can promote a feeling of closeness and security in the known response of available adults (Dunn 1993). Some parents may benefit from opportunities to have shared fun with their children, for example on outings.

3. Any activity which promotes a sense of shared fun is important as some children will have experienced little pleasure in play or other activities and little sense of enjoying themselves. Any ordinary play experience can provide opportunities for this, for example, water play, modelling with clay, and so on.

4. As children's attachment relationships improve, so they should begin to show more discrimination between known and unknown adults. But if they do not, then all adults who come into contact with the child should be advised to model appropriate behaviour, for example, if a child jumps onto the social worker's lap on the first meeting the worker can say; 'I think we should check whether mum/dad/carer is happy for you to sit on my lap – you ask them'. When meeting new people the parent or carer can use phrases such as 'Now, you don't know XX very well yet, but if we chat a bit we can get to know them better' and so on. Care must be taken to protect such children from unscrupulous adults.

5. The parent or carer should take every opportunity, not only to *respond* to a child's demonstrated distress and to support him or her when under stress but also to *reach out* to the child to initiate positive experiences (Fahlberg 1991). It is not helpful simply to wait for the child to voice concerns, as many children will find this too difficult. It is vital that the carer or parent takes initiatives to protect the child from undue negative effects of adverse circumstances.

6. When trying to understand any messages the child may be giving about his or her assumptions as to why he or she is not at home, why someone important has left, or the reasons for any other negative life events, help the parent or carer to reflect upon the child's *behaviour*, as well as what he or she *says*. Initiatives that encourage *reflection* with the child about the reasons for decisions or life events can be powerfully protective against later difficulties because self-blame is developmentally likely at these early ages.

7. At this stage of development individual programmes involving art, music and play therapy programmes can be extremely helpful. Many young children explore through their play experiences events that have troubled them or about which they feel great confusion. An opportunity for the child to lead the play can promote the communication of his or her worries and confusions and give the adult an opportunity to understand what the child has made of previous life events.

8. Any way in which the adult can communicate an *acceptance* to a very young child of their individuality is likely to be of great value. For example, simple activities like drawing around the child's body outline on paper and colouring in the child's particular features can provide an opportunity for positive acknowledgement of his or her attributes.

9. Respectful nurturing touch from adults is likely to be very reassuring for the young child. Non-abusive, nurturing touch can be deeply comforting to a child who has had physical or sexually abusive experiences. The importance of physical care is clear, not only in the provision of nourishing food, but also helping the child to care for him or herself in a simple way. Equally the provision of reliable medical attention for particular needs or conditions that may have been neglected gives positive messages to the child and offers chances for physical closeness.

Ensuring that the child has a secure base

1. Building healthier attachment relationships may be the most important initiative which, through work with parent and child separately or the parent and child relationship directly, can make a real difference to the child's sense of security. An essential element of a secure base for very young children is predictability of care. Steady routines can have a deeply reassuring affect and the reliable availability of those important to the child provides a sense of belonging. Children need a balance between, on the one hand healthy limit setting and predictable routines of care and, on the other encouragement to take initiatives and explore the environment safely. The right balance here will also promote healthy initiative and assertion, forming the basis of sound cognitive development through play and exploration. Spend time with the parent or carer exploring the caring routines. For example, particular attention can be paid to providing enjoyable meal times as in some families these have been fraught occasions for the young children. Bedtimes can also be comforting times for enjoyable routines, for example, having a bath and reading a story.

2. For many children who are insecure, for those who have separated from important adults, and particularly for children whose development is delayed, experiences geared at *exploring the senses* can be powerfully therapeutic. Sensory experiences are the way in which young children experience the world and play opportunities of this kind, for example, using dough, paints, water, music can be deeply reassuring. These can be helpful ways of relaxing very anxious children and beginning to teach them simple ways of calming themselves which will be an invaluable personal resource in later life.

3. Interest in the child's activities, encouragement of the child to take initiatives in play and development of the child's autonomy, will also build self-esteem.

4. The child who has difficulty separating needs to develop trust in the carer which can be encouraged by leaving the child for short periods with a known adult. At first the carer may go only into another room. As the child's trust grows, so longer separations can occur. The child should not be 'tricked' by the carer disappearing without any explanation.

5.   Any play experience which can be constructed by a trusted adult to help a child to anticipate a difficult experience, and to play it out using objects of any kind, can help the child prepare him or herself for a stressful event. For example, for the child who is going to hospital it can help greatly to use the natural medium of play to predict some of the experiences the child is likely to have, and to offer reassurance. Encouragement to take a special toy and to be reassured of the availability of important adults will protect against the young child's sense of powerlessness and anxiety. It can also provide an opportunity for the expression of feelings that can be legitimised and supported by the adult.

6.   Taking opportunities for special rituals for each individual child, at Christmas or other religious festivals, on their birthday and in celebration of significant achievements or events can build a trusting relationship between the child and a significant adult.

7.   Any initiative and work with parents which helps them to learn about the developmental stage and actions they can take to increase the child's sense of security will be invaluable. For example, reliable, predictable routines are often underestimated by parents who themselves have had poor experiences of nurturing and group work support can help parents to understand about children's needs. It is likely that a combination of interventions that encourage direct positive engagement with the children in structured play sessions or nurturing tasks, with an opportunity for reflection with other parents is likely to be more successful than either initiative on its own. One approach to group work focuses on helping parents to change the kind of attributions they make about their children's behaviour.

8.   Any initiative, however small, which communicates to the child that the adult has *space* and *time* for him or her and that they are unique and special in their own way, is likely to communicate a message of positive regard. Predictable periods of time spent with the child by a caring adult offering praise and encouragement and affirmation can be of vital significance, for example, by the regular telling of stories or engaging in special activities that have meaning for the individual child.

9.   Whatever the child's living setting, he or she will need the comfort of contact with important people from his or her past and present: to have a notion that 'I have adults available to me when I need them'. Contact, if the child is separated from attachment figures, needs to be *purposeful*

so that it aims to meet the child's needs. It is also important to consult with the family about *how* contact can be prepared for and effectively managed. Many parents find it very difficult to be in a false setting for contact with their child, so careful consideration of venue, activities and timing will be important in promoting the most effective contact for the child. Active gaining of *permission* from parents is vital here, even if it takes time, as it can consolidate the secure base both in the present placement and future care settings if the child knows that the parent is able to communicate their approval.

10. Take photographs of important shared experiences to provide a sense of continuity for the child and reminders of important people and experiences. Photographs, tapes, drawings and videos can all help to keep important memories of life for the child and remind him or her of their roots and sense of belonging in their community.

11. More work may need to be done with the adults, for example, when there are warring, separated parents, than directly with the children in establishing the child's right to contact with an important person who has left the household.

Capitalising upon the wider resources that are available as an attachment network

1. Enjoyable outings with a trusted adult can extend the child's world, giving him or her an opportunity to explore the environment and increasing the range of stimulation.

2. Base deliberate plans for care and contact upon careful attention to children's wishes and feelings to counteract both feelings of powerlessness and those of self-blame. Take care in thinking through with the child wherever possible *who* is important so that opportunities to sustain and build important attachments can be maintained, despite separations.

3. It may be that important people to the child are overlooked when making the care plan, or their significance minimised. It may be assumed that the child's mother is more important when a grandparent or father may be of real significance. Make no assumptions about who has something to offer the child.

4. Assess the nature and strength of sibling bonds and reassess this in the light of reparative work

and care. For example, for a sibling group where conflict has been a necessary adaptation to difficult family circumstances, or where there is an unhelpful allocation of roles to individual children, special attention to building mutual empathy may be invaluable. For example, an older sibling who completely takes over a younger child as a result of poor overall nurturing of all the children can be released from this responsibility. The aims here might be:

(a) rewarding 'required helpfulness', while

(b) encouraging the older child to relinquish elements of the caring role which detract from their own healthy development, and

(c) encouraging age appropriate initiatives for the older child and assertion in the younger child.

5. Resources available to support parents of young children within the community can be vital sources of help, especially for isolated, vulnerable parents. Consideration needs to be given to the parent's current personal resources when making plans for support initiatives. For example, where parents are depressed, making new social links may be very difficult for them, so keeping support initiatives focused and confined helps to minimise the emotional demands on them (Thompson 1995).

6. Ensure that the parents are provided with the financial and material resources that they need to support them in their parenting. This will include ensuring that all due benefits are applied for, that the housing department keeps the house upgraded, that training and job opportunities are available and so on.

7. The search for somewhere permanent to stay for the child, if the living arrangements are uncertain, or if the child has experienced a previous separation, is of vital significance in confirming a sense of a secure base. For the child who is separated from family, it is very important to search for significant family members who may not only be parents or grandparents. For example, even for children who come from families where abuse is endemic, it is often possible to find an extended family member who has survived these difficulties and who can act as a positive role model for the child. Facilitating contact with any important person to the child promotes a sense of continuity and therefore strengthens the sense of secure base.

8. For the child who is at home, it may be that there is an important neighbour who can be encouraged to have consistent nurturing individual contact with the child.

9. Try to organise for continuity of availability of any professionals involved with the child.

10. Playgroups and nurseries can provide invaluable sources of stimulation, care and nourishment and emotional support for vulnerable young children. Consideration should be given to the culture which is established within the setting, so that not only does it welcome the children in a nurturing fashion, but also it is inclusive and respectful towards their parents and extended family members.

11. For children who come from minority ethnic or cultural groups, it is vitally important that the links with their culture remain wherever possible. These links need to be given positive value by those caring for children from different communities if they have to be separated from their birth and extended families. Involvement of the child in familiar religious or cultural events or routines can reassure the child that his or her origins are valued by those caring for them. Such rituals as the preparation of familiar foods give powerful positive messages about the child's culture.

12. If staff feel uncertain of their knowledge of particular cultural practices of families whose children they are caring for and working with, it is helpful if agencies take initiatives to equip carers and workers to make positive overtures towards families so that what is offered to the child and family is respectful of culture and tradition. For example, it would be easy to make the assumption that a mother always plays with a child, based on Eurocentric assumptions, whereas in some communities it may well be the older sibling who undertakes more playful interaction with the child or perhaps an aunt, uncle or grandparent.

13. Every opportunity needs to be taken with young children in communicating an acceptance of *difference*. This is especially important for children who come from minority social groupings and therefore may already be experiencing prejudice and even rejection. The City of Bradford Metropolitan Council recommends the adoption of techniques with children under 5 who are black or of mixed parentage that can be used in promoting a positive sense of black identity:

(a) When bathing the young child, even if the child has no speech, talking to him or her and pointing out parts of the body, for example, 'You've got beautiful black fingers'. White staff can show the child the difference by placing their own hand alongside.

(b) It is essential to have black images or models or at least black people in posters involved in a wide range of occupations and activities. Too many nurseries fall short in this respect. It is unacceptable to have young children brought up without any exposure to a variety of cultures. To aim to nurture a young black child's personality in all-white establishments with white models in posters is highly questionable.

(c) It is important to refrain from statements like this one, even as a joke, 'Have you really washed your face and hands? I have no way of telling if they are really clean'. As simple as the above sounds, and it is said so often by some adults, it can begin the erosion of a young black child's identity. Many young children who view themselves as dirty and display a diminished display of self-esteem have associated blackness with dirt.

(d) In response to a direct question by a 3- or 4-year-old, such as 'Am I white or black?', it is important to associate the answer with a positive black person in the child's life, for example, 'Yes, black like Mummy or Jean who looks after you'. A child exposed to positive references about him or herself from confident caretakers is more likely to develop a secure personality.

(e) For those separated children who come from families where English is not spoken as a first language, it can be of particular value to maintain contact with the child's extended family and community. It is also helpful to look for a befriender or mentor who can engage with the child to continue with positive messages about his or her culture.

PRACTICE SUGGESTIONS
EDUCATION

Much can be learned from children and family centres as to ideas for promoting healthy development within this domain. The attitude of staff in a nursery or a family centre setting will be vital in either encouraging or discouraging parents' direct involvement. It is most important to remember to attempt to engage fathers as well as mothers in

any work being undertaken with a very young child and some suggestions for how to do this are included below (see also Daniel and Taylor 2001).

It is vital to be able to encourage as much flexibility as possible, particularly when one is working with a community of parents whose available time does not fit regular schedules.

An open-minded approach to families of different cultures, as well as those representative of the dominant culture, will inform good practice.

Helping the child to develop curiosity about his or her environment

1. The communication of sustained interest in every achievement, however small can help encourage curiosity. Find simple ways of acknowledging and celebrating achievements. Keep photographs of shared experiences with the child, particularly when they involve mastery of signs of increasing competence. The making of simple certificates or medals to signify success is helpful.

2. Exploration can be encouraged by ordinary activities like storytelling or baking, but can also include special activities, for example outings. Use games which include the development of effective developmental progress geared to the individual child's needs, for example, for the very passive child who is reluctant to explore, choose a programme of activities to kindle the child's imagination and involve gradually extending periods of exploration and play. Model safe boundaries around play activities to enhance the child's confidence in exploring without putting them at risk.

3. Self-esteem can be promoted by encouraging the child to undertake special tasks carrying importance for the family or the children's group.

4. Talking and reading with the child promote the comprehension and use of language. Even very young children can be taken to libraries and bookshops to choose books.

5. Concentration can be encouraged within a context of quality special time with a caring adult, offering encouragement and praise to the child.

6. Provide stimulating experiences that enhance the child's awareness of their senses, for example, water play, music and simple storytelling and role play stimulate pretend play.

7. The availability of soft play materials allows the letting off of steam in a safe environment. Communicate to young children that there are ways in which they can express any anger they feel, as many children may feel full of anger and confusion at the experiences they have endured.

Helping to enhance the parent or carer environment so that it facilitates the child's cognitive development

1. There should be a non-threatening and nurturing series of opportunities for parents to gain new skills in playing with their children. Encourage parents to attend to the child's play in a respectful manner, to be sensitive to the child's own style of play and encourage them to follow this without interrupting or criticising or challenging the child. This is particularly helpful when a relationship between a parent and a very young child is in real trouble. In addition to this, attention to parents' wishes and feelings, memories of past life events, particularly attachment experiences, and immediate distressing problems in their own lives will help the parents to attend to their own child's needs for play and stimulation.

2. The initial relationship building is crucial in engaging parents in providing rich play opportunities for their children. Every contact we have with parents communicates a message as to the importance of them in the process and it is wise to begin with the positives, however apparently small, rather than focusing on negatives and problems. The parent will then be in a better position to help the child concentrate on activities.

3.   Some parents had, themselves, impoverished experiences of play and may need a parallel or even preliminary opportunity to explore and enjoy play activities themselves before they can offer these opportunities to their young children.

4.   For some parents, who have never had any kind of creative opportunity, it may be necessary to begin with allowing them a creative opportunity for themselves, bridging the use of this with their own children over time.

5.   When helping parents to encourage their children, it is wise to identify small, achievable tasks if the parent is reluctant or fearful. Any ideas that the parent has should be respected. Some parents have unrealistic expectations of what young children can achieve and may benefit from information about child development. Health visitors can help with this.

6.   If parents are unable or unwilling to read to the child then ensure that someone else does.

7.   It may be very difficult, partly because of the mainly female and child nature of many pre-school environments, to encourage fathers to be actively involved in the pre-school setting. Many opportunities can be lost through not making particular extra efforts to invite fathers to take part in a constructive manner. Exploring with them their interests, skills and abilities and the contribution they may make to involvement with other parents, as well as with their own child, may be helpful preparation for this participation. In some cases where a father has been violent or abusive towards the mother or child it may be necessary to mediate the father's involvement in some circumstances. Suggestions of practice include:

(a)   More male workers as role models within pre-school settings.

(b)   Men's groups supporting fathers from whatever base they feel they have a contribution to make.

(c)   Direct work with mothers to deal with possible resistance to fathers' involvement.

(d)   A positive attitude towards fathers' ideas, recognition of their contribution and celebration of this.

(e)   Strategies to make men feel more comfortable in a mainly female and child environment.

(f)   Home-based strategies with fathers to encourage play.

(g)   Opportunities to spend time in the playroom with other fathers, or alone to encourage their confidence in play.

(h)   Involving fathers in any meetings to consider the use of pre-school resources.

(i)   Listening to fathers' wishes and feelings in relation to their children.

(j)   Supporting the child directly in making an attachment to his or her father.

(k)   Giving the child opportunities to talk about the father.

(l)   Encouraging regular and consistent contact for fathers with the pre-school setting.

(m)   Encouraging fathers' involvement in planning and decision-making, for example around case conferences.

(n)   Encouraging members of the father's extended family to contribute to the child's well-being.

Exploring wider opportunities for cognitive stimulation

1.   There may be opportunities within the child's extended family and other natural network for stimulating contact with other children. If there are no such naturally occurring opportunities then more formal settings can be considered, for example, a day-care placement with other children.

2.   Some parents feel that children must have expensive toys and feel inadequate if they cannot afford to provide them. They need reassurance that stimulating toys need not be expensive: all sorts of household items and boxes and so on can be used to stimulate imaginative play. In some cases, however, it may be helpful to provide finance for specific items, particularly interesting, age-appropriate books.

3.   If there are any local toy libraries and libraries help parents to access initial registration.

4. Any local groups or activities for children in the community should be considered. Many areas have activity clubs for young children and parents may need help with finance to allow their child to attend.

5. It is important to look as widely as possible within the extended family for an older child or adult who is willing to spend some time encouraging the child's learning and cognitive development.

6. There is an increase in family-based initiatives within the community aimed at supporting parents and their vulnerable young children. Because many parents are themselves isolated, it is important to make available to them user-friendly resources so as to build their own social links and supports, as well as offering an opportunity for the nourishment of the positives in the relationship with their child. These can be an important resource to prepare vulnerable young children for the school setting and all associated significant changes.

7. Local projects involving voluntary agencies, for example, Homestart and projects funded by Barnardos or National Children's Homes (NCH) Action for Children increasingly focus on specific play resources in the local community. These can help many vulnerable young children by making available opportunities for stimulation and play and equally by supporting their parents in group or individual work, to engage in play activities with their children in a positive way.

8. It is very important that parents are encouraged to feel safe in the pre-school setting and to feel that they have something to contribute through life at home as well as their activities in the pre-school setting itself. It may well be most helpful to introduce parents to other parents who have experienced similar issues and dilemmas with their own children as this will probably be immensely supportive to them. It also may be necessary to accompany parents to local resource groups to ease them in to involvement.

PRACTICE SUGGESTIONS
FRIENDSHIPS

Helping the child to develop the characteristics that help with making and keeping friends

1. If a young child is excessively shy, he or she will need gentle encouragement and support with peer interactions. The child is likely to find large play groups or nurseries overwhelming; instead he or she may benefit from regular contact with one or two other children that the child can become familiar with. Within the family network, there may be a relative who also has a young child and who would be willing to see the child on a regular basis and supervise play activities. Or, a placement with a day carer who also looks after one or two other children could provide contact on a regular basis with known children.

2. If a child is excessively aggressive towards other children at a young age then he or she needs direct, clear, appropriate and firm adult intervention at points of conflict. The Positive Values domain provides further ideas about the encouragement of kind behaviour towards others.

3. Use dolls, drawings, toys and/or photos of other known children to help a child who finds it hard to identify his or her friends. Encourage him or her to think about what he or she enjoys doing and who they might like to share activities with. If the child does have an idea about who his or her friend is, then this can be used as a basis for developing talents and interests as joint activities can be planned.

4. Similarly, use dolls, drawings, photos and so on to help the child's understanding of the concept of friendship. For example, he or she can be encouraged to think about all the things that can be done with other children, for example, some games cannot be played without other children.

5. If the child does have a good concept of friendship, then this is a good basis upon which to build positive values and talents and interests. Consider involving other children in joint activities and outings.

6. If the child is attending a formal day-care setting then there will be numerous opportunities to attend to issues of peer relationships in general and friendships in particular.

Encouraging a parent or carer environment that facilitates the development of friendship

1. It is not uncommon for parents to underestimate the benefits to young children of spending time with other children. In such circumstances parents may need advice and guidance about the value of such contact and about how to organise it. If at all possible, encourage parents to build upon naturally occurring contact with relatives and friends and their children.

2. Children who are referred because of neglect often have parents who are isolated and lack friends. Because young children are highly dependent upon their parents for contact with other children, the knock-on effect of parental isolation is restricted contact with peers. Parents of neglected children also have a tendency to perceive themselves as more lonely and lacking in support, perhaps because of low self-esteem and self-efficacy. Therefore, intervention may need to focus upon helping the parent to make more satisfactory friendships themselves. Parents who are anxious about making contact with others may find it easier to do so via their children, through parent and toddler groups for example.

3. If there are no local parent–toddler groups in the area, parents can be encouraged to get together and start one. Many such groups are focused exclusively upon mothers, so consider encouraging fathers to be involved with their child's friendships.

4. Parents may need advice about how best to intervene when disputes occur among young children. The Positive Values domain has more suggestions on this.

5. Some difficulties with friendships are rooted in attachment problems, and these can be addressed by using suggestions from the Secure Base domain.

Helping with the child's current friendships

1. If at all possible, make use of naturally occurring opportunities for the child to have contact with other children. For example, a grandparent's house can act as a base for cousins to meet and play, uncles and aunts can be encouraged to include their nieces and nephews in activities and outings, older siblings may have friends who also have younger siblings who could be a source of friends and neighbours may have young children.

2. If there are no natural resources that can be built upon or enhanced and supported, then consider mainstream activities such as toddlers' groups, play groups, school nurseries, gymnastics for little children, swimming classes, soft-play centres and so on.

3. Finally, a referral can be made to a formal child-care setting such as a children's or family centre.

4. If children are to be accommodated away from home, or are to change placement, do not assume that their current friendships are not important to them. Respect friendships that they have already made, allow them to continue if possible, otherwise enable the child to say goodbye properly, perhaps by drawing a card. Arrange for the child to have photos of friends.

PRACTICE SUGGESTIONS
TALENTS AND INTERESTS

If there is already an area of strength it will be important to capitalise on established skills. However, in the work with many children, established talents and abilities may not be readily apparent in the work and intervention should focus on how the child's potential abilities can be explored.

The case studies at the end of the workbook illustrate the potential for using an ability or talent to support a healthy sense of identity in a young person who has experienced not only abuse but also many separations and losses. It will be seen from the examples that some children and young people who avoid intimacy with caring adults or who are ambivalent, can experience the support of adults over time in developing a set of talents. This, less obviously than in direct attempts to bring the child to accept caring overtures, can build the child's ability to depend healthily on those caring for them.

Therefore, this domain links closely with the notion of children being able to say 'I can' in relation to their own capacities. It also helps to build a sense of identity in exploring and establishing, not only competencies, but also a sense of identity rooted in a unique collection of attributes. In this way, the 'I can' contributes to the ' I am' or what can be seen as self-esteem.

Encouraging the child in his or her particular talents and interests

1. A great deal of persistence may be required in finding a particular talent or ability in an individual child. Because many children have a natural lack of confidence, particularly if they have been ignored or discouraged, great tenacity can be required to communicate the belief in the child's ability by maintaining effort, even in the face of the child's passivity and apparent diffidence. Use simple ways to encourage the child's imaginative ability, for example, by building a story together with an adult, taking turns to develop the storyline and so on.

2. Use of drama is particularly powerful with children who may have learned to suppress powerful feelings. For example, use a dressing-up box full of clothes that the young child can readily use to adopt different roles. This not only develops the child's capacity for imagination, but also may act as an opportunity for the replaying of powerful difficult or enjoyable memories.

3. Young children who are delayed in their development require very active encouragement. The young child who is very passive needs his or her carers to persist in offering stimulation to explore the environment. The uncontrolled, highly impulsive young child needs safe boundaries within which he or she can gradually explore the environment and begin to play.

4. Talents and natural abilities or potential may be seen from ordinary activities and may become apparent during the course of play activities, either structured or spontaneous. Play is young children's work in that it is the means through which young children both explore and make sense of the world. Some children who have been profoundly neglected, however, will be slow to take any initiative in play and may

be preoccupied with maintaining closeness with the adult. Gradually from this base, as the child becomes more confident, play activities can become an important pleasurable feature of the child's daily life.

5. Encouraging all kinds of play is helpful in promoting a sense of initiative, the precursor to healthy assertion and exploration. For example:

    (a) role play

    (b) imaginative play

    (c) playing house

    (d) play involving the care of a young baby which can build a sense of security.

6. The natural style of the child's play, the activities to which he or she is spontaneously drawn, can tell us much about the abilities and capacities that can be nurtured to considerable effect. For example, some children are very physical in their play and use their bodies with agility. This can be encouraged as a basis for the later development of the physical coordination necessary for all kinds of sports, dance, gymnastics or other hobbies.

7. Other children may naturally choose to express themselves using their hands, for example in using clay, modelling clay or in drawing. Use play activities to encourage this to promote the extension of this natural inclination towards the acquisition of skills.

8. Children who find relief from tension, pleasure or relaxation from building models or shaping anything in their world, can, with encouragement, develop abilities so that the skills form the basis of a hobby. This can equip the young child with a mode of expression for expressing *feelings* and is, therefore, of potential therapeutic value.

9. Carefully nurture ability in an enjoyable way to provide:

    (a) the chance for the child to enjoy themselves

    (b) opportunities for mastering achievement

    (c) a chance to celebrate their involvement in everything at nursery and playgroup.

10. Develop playful activities that explore and develop the child's use of the senses to fill in gaps in the child's developmental experiences. For example, it may be helpful to think of simple games that explore the

senses of seeing, touching, smelling and hearing. For example, put together a box of articles with particular fragrances that not only can be a source of enjoyment for the child in discovering new smells, but also can operate as a basis to distinguish likes and dislikes for the first time. Ideas such as a 'treasure box' can also be useful in work with young children who have not had the opportunity to explore different textures of objects. The box can contain anything that represents different textures, for example, velvet, spiky objects and cotton wool, and the child is left to explore these objects so as develop sensory abilities.

11. Some children with disabilities can excel in particular areas and this may need persistent interest by at least one caring adult to discover and then support the talent or ability. A talent can give a child a vehicle for expressing feelings, for example:

   (a)   cartoon drawing

   (b)   computer skills

   (c)   design or artistic skills.

Ensuring that the parent or carer environment supports the development of talents and interests

   1.   Involvement in a favourite hobby or talent may be a useful focus for meaningful involvement of fathers with their children, including those in circumstances of marital or partner separation.

   2.   It is helpful for the adult to concentrate on following the young child's play, commenting upon it and allowing the child to take the lead. This is the basic method used in the therapeutic technique the 'parent/child game' in which 10 minutes of cooperative play is encouraged between parent and child (Forehand and McMahon 1981). The emphasis here is on strengthening the elements of play and encouragement from the adult to the young child. The parent is encouraged to avoid:

   (a)   interference

   (b)   criticism

   (c)   the adult taking over the initiative

   (d)   diverting the child's attention.

This promotes the child's sense of initiative through which he or she discovers skills and abilities, and promotes pleasure in the relationship and cooperation rather than resistance.

3. An awareness of what soothes and comforts children as well as what frightens and distresses them can be invaluable in supporting a child to take part in a range of activities. For example, one foster carer helped a very young child to separate from her for very brief periods by spraying her own perfume on the child's hankie prior to the separation. The child could then comfort herself with the reassurance of the familiar fragrance. This helped the young child to make the transition into and through the separation.

4. A sensitive young child may need active support. Model healthy exploration and various kinds of play for example, by saying 'I'll go first and then it's your turn'.

5. Parents may need support to believe in their own abilities to help their child to develop a talent or a skill. For example, if they have had poor experiences of play in their own childhood they may be at a loss as to how to create opportunities for play for their young child. It may well be constructive to support parents individually or in groups to enjoy play opportunities for themselves and to rediscover or find out for the first time their own skills and capacities.

6. Parents and carers can support the child powerfully through their interest in a particular natural ability, for example:

    (a) playing ball with a young child to help him or her to learn simple coordination skills

    (b) singing with a child, teaching simple songs to form part of the daily routine of play

    (c) rehearsing or modelling physical release of tension involved in lively play such as running or swimming

    (d) rehearsing a dance with a child as well as accompanying them to a class.

7. These shared activities can incidentally provide many opportunities for intimacy in a less direct way, for example, teaching a reluctant or avoidant child to swim can encourage him or her to depend on adults more than he or she would otherwise choose.

Drawing upon opportunities in the wider community to nurture the child's talents and interests

1. Extended family members can be helpful in offering regular play opportunities, for example, trips to the swing park.

2. Many young children need support to make links with other children. Not every young child is immediately sociable. Depending on past adverse experiences, young children may react in different ways to play opportunities. Some of the problems may be those of:

   (a) passive withdrawal

   (b) clinging to the protection of the attachment figure

   (c) domination of other children

   (d) inability to share activities.

   Therefore, tailor play activities to the child's temperament.

3. It is probably unhelpful to assume each child must enjoy peer play by a particular stage of development but there can be pleasure for some children in playing alongside another child, following on usually from a period of support in shared play with an adult.

4. Nurseries, toddlers' groups, and other clubs and activities for young children vary in the extent to which they aim to nurture an individual child's talents. Involve parents in a joint endeavour to find out what is available locally.

5. Children from minority cultures can find a secure base in activities linked with their own cultural heritage, for example dance or key position in religious observance to rituals. Finding an adult to act as a mentor from the child's natural networks in the community is particularly important here.

PRACTICE SUGGESTIONS
POSITIVE VALUES

Helping this child develop moral reasoning and to understand his or her own feelings and empathise with those of people close to them

1. The pictures 'Emotional faces' provided to help with the assessment of this domain can also be used to help children who have difficulty in recognising and labelling emotions of their own or other people. In some cases the child may simply need to learn the vocabulary of feelings.

2. Children learn much about emotions through play. Play sessions with other children can be arranged and supervised and the adult can make simple comments that label the emotions. For example, if a chasing game is organised, the one running away can act out fear. With imagination a whole range of games and role plays can be devised that involve emotions.

3. Use the 'theory of mind' tasks in the Positive Values domain to help the child with perspective-taking. The child could be actively encouraged to visualise what the child in the task sees. Other tasks that are specific to that child's experience could be developed.

4. Cuddly toys and dolls can be used to help with perspective-taking. For example, a teddy can be placed in another part of the room and the child asked to describe what the teddy can see, before going to check.

5. The cartoons provided for assessment can be used to help the child consider how others might react in different situations. Practitioners can work with carers and parents to devise similar scenarios tailored to the child's experience. Whenever possible, any opportunities to explore ways in which different people may have different reactions to the same

situation should be used, for example, some children find swinging high exciting, whereas others find it frightening.

6. Use any opportunities to demonstrate empathy towards the child and others. Simple statements such as 'Sometimes children feel sad when … is that how you feel?' can be helpful.

7. Initiate active conversations about how someone else may be feeling. Use pets also in this context, for example, '[This cat] likes to be stroked under the chin, but some cats like their ears tickled' or '[This dog] enjoys chasing after balls, but other dogs like catching sticks'.

Encouraging the child to help others

1. Encourage the parent or carer to recognise, accept and praise any verbal offers of help or apparent attempts to help. If parents are tired and stressed, it may be hard for them to keep patience with a child's slow and perhaps clumsy efforts. In these cases it might be helpful to spend some time with them working out a series of simple 'chores' for the child to do.

2. In some cases there may be concern that a young child is expected to help too much. In these cases the aim has to be to find a happy medium and, if necessary, to arrange for the child to have respite in day care or a nursery.

3. Because of their extensive experience of child care, many foster parents will want to ask children to help with chores. There may be anxieties about how much is appropriate, especially if a child has been expected to carry out too much work at home. The appropriate amount of required helpfulness can be discussed in planning discussions so that all involved can agree on a level.

4. Most helping behaviour of very young children is carried out in the home and therefore the parent or carer is likely to be the main resource. If children consistently refuse to help, it may be because the manner in which they are asked is unhelpful, or because they simply do not understand what is requested of them. Sometimes it might be helpful to provide a set of toy household items for the child to use in imitation of the parent.

5. When there is no appropriate support for a child's helping behaviour in the home, and the likelihood of this changing is minimal, then look for other people in the child's network who appear to have the patience to help, for example, grandparents could be encouraged to ask the child to help them with simple tasks, such as tidying up, weeding, cleaning the car, carrying shopping, making beds. If a regular arrangement can be made, all the better.

6. Instead of taking the child out, the social worker could sometimes arrange joint activities in the home, for example baking, or making a picture for the wall.

Encouraging the child to show comforting, sharing and more general prosocial behaviour

1. The ideal way for children to learn positive behaviour is by imitation. All interactions with the child should therefore model caring and comforting. Again the parent or carer has to be the main resource here. Parents may need advice and support to actively encourage comforting and sharing behaviour between siblings and the child and other children.

2. Young children should be given clear rules and boundaries about behaviour towards others and any signs of cruelty, unkindness or hurting to other children or adults should be stopped.

3. Any spontaneous act of sharing or kindness should be praised and reinforced. Parents may need advice on how best to do this.

4. Contact with pets and animals can help with the development of kindness. If it is not appropriate for there to be a pet in the household, there may be opportunities for children to help with a relative or neighbour's pet. Trips to city farms or zoos with pets' corners that allow animal handling may also help.

5. Very young children who need help with this domain could benefit from a place in a small, nurturing family centre, nursery or day-care placement. If a child is already showing active signs of cruelty to others, then his or her behaviour will require a high level of monitoring by skilled staff who can intervene as quickly as possible with firm and clear messages against harm to others.

6.   Young children need to have contact with their peers in order to learn about cooperative play and sharing toys. Ensure that the child has access to some form of formal or informal contact with other children that is supervised by an adult skilled in facilitating cooperative play.

7.   Children live up to the attributions ascribed to them, so whenever appropriate they need to hear that they are good and kind: 'That was kind of you to…'

PRACTICE SUGGESTIONS
SOCIAL COMPETENCIES

There are a number of commercially available packs and books that give suggestions for intervention with social competence and related behaviour with young children.

Bruce and Meggit's *Child Care and Education* is a useful reference for practitioners that has sections on social and emotional development and feelings and relationships (Bruce and Meggit 1999).

The Open University's pack *Confident Parents: Confident Children* is widely used as a guide to developing effective parenting and will be helpful both for practitioners advising parents and for direct use by parents (Open University 1997).

Willow and Hoyder's book *It Hurts You Inside* describes research by Save the Children on children's views about why adults smack and contains children's accounts of how it makes them feel (Willow and Hoyder 1998).

Derman-Sparks' *Anti-Bias Curriculum: Tools for Empowering Young Children* contain group work material for use by professionals for looking at issues of discrimination. As there is evidence that tolerance of individual differences is associated with resilience this may be a helpful approach for some children (Derman-Sparks 1989).

Helping the child to develop the personal characteristics that help with social competence

Many of these characteristics are associated with security of attachment. For example, if the child is insecurely attached to the parent or carer (as assessed in Secure Base domain), then he or she is likely to have problems with autonomy, either showing too much or too little. It is through early

attachment relationships that young children learn many of the fundamentals of social competence. Therefore, if secure attachment relationships can be fostered, they should be the primary locus of work on social competence. However, lack of social competence can also impede the development of new attachments, so if the child is lacking in this domain, it may be helpful for future attachment to ensure that reparative work is carried out, even in the absence of a secure attachment.

AUTONOMY

Provide parents with information about child development to help them understand the reasons why young children try to assert their own personality. Explore with parents the kind of autonomy that they can encourage in their child, for example making simple choices between two options; being encouraged to lead games and activities and so on. The child's individual preferences can be encouraged, even on simple things like his or her favourite colour, toy or drink. During all direct contact with the child he or she should be involved in as much decision-making as possible.

SELF-CONTROL

If the young child is showing excessive aggression then it should not be assumed that he or she will 'grow out of it'. Simple behavioural techniques, with the use of time-out as a sanction and praise as reinforcement of appropriate behaviour, can be very effective. Consider using alternative day care where there is a good adult–child ratio and a culture of warmth and prompt intervention with aggression.

TEMPERAMENT

There is evidence that differences in temperament can be exhibited at a very young age (Buss and Plomin 1984; Chess and Thomas 1977) and having a positive easy temperament is a major factor in promoting resilience. For a child with a less easy temperament the most effective care is that which meshes with the child. If a parent withdraws from a difficult child and is critical, then the child is likely to become even more difficult. The parent or carer should be encouraged to continue to show affection for the child, while dealing with the problem behaviour (Santrok 1994). If looking for alternative full-time or day carers, then attention has to be paid to the 'fit' between adult and child temperament.

SELF-EFFICACY

Young children who have been neglected or abused frequently develop attributions for events as out of their control, likely to remain negative and as being global. This can make them very reluctant to try new tasks, because they believe that they will fail. The experience of positive events, such as an enjoyable outing, the concentrated attention of a liked adult and so on, can help to change this view that good things will not happen to them.

The child has to be encouraged to try simple tasks at which he or she can succeed. This requires skill on behalf of the helper to manipulate situations so that the child tries something almost before realising it. Nursery staff are the obvious people to enlist with help in this.

He or she also then needs to learn that some tasks are not within his or her range and that this is not their fault. They could be taken to a park that has apparatus with a lower age limit, these can be used to illustrate that little children are just too little for them; similarly, swimming pools with pools for toddlers can be used to show the same. Adults can also model the fact that there are some tasks that are beyond them.

ATTENTION

Try to find a member of the child's network who is prepared to spend some concentrated time with the child on a regular occasion. An older sibling might be able to do this. A number of activities can be suggested:

1. Encourage and reward the child for looking at you when you talk to him or her.

2. Move to the child's level and engage his or her attention and talk to him or her about things that interest him or her, all the while praising him or her for listening.

3. Find a game he or she likes and play it regularly, increasing the length of time you encourage him or her to play each time and praising the child.

4. Use videos with very short stories or cartoons, and move onto increasingly longer videos, watch them with the child and engage in joint attention to details.

5. Find very short stories to read right through and make coming to the end an exciting occasion. If he or she needs a break, pick up where you left off and continue to the end.

6. Use drawing, colouring and other activities to encourage concentration.

7. Use stories to help children attend to cause and effect.

8. Make sure that you listen to things that children try to tell you, show that you are interested in hearing what they have to say, ask them further questions about what they are telling you, draw other members of the family into the conversation.

Helping the parent or carer to provide an environment that encourages social competence

1. Work with the parent or carer to devise a list of social competencies that they would like to see their child develop. Help them to develop strategies, based upon reward, for their encouragement. For example, praise for responding quickly when spoken to or for saying please and thank you.

2. Authoritative parenting incorporates both warmth and consistent boundaries. Parents may well benefit from the opportunity to attend a parenting group where they can share their experiences with others and consider different ways of encouraging social competence in their children.

3. When parents themselves lack social competence and perhaps condone their children's behaviour, then look for an alternative role model for the child for example, a member of the extended family, a mentor, volunteer, nursery worker or day carer.

Helping the child to develop competence in a wider social environment

1. Ensure that the child has contact with other children, either by an informal arrangement between a group of parents, or in a formal nursery or family centre setting.

2. If a child has a problem with his or her interactions with other children then adult supervision of play is essential.

3. The child who lacks confidence will need the opportunity for unthreatening contact with adults in whom they can develop trust. The

child who is over-confident with total strangers will need to be taught the difference between known and unknown people.

4.   An example of a technique for teaching social competence to young children is the Interpersonal Cognitive Problem-solving Program (ICPS) (Spivak and Shure 1974), which is described in comprehensive detail by Goldstein . The aim is to help parents to teach children how to think, not what to think, in other words to help them learn about problem-solving, rather than providing the solutions (1999). The formal programme is too detailed to set out here, but it involves using puppets, dolls and other toys to recreate problem situations and teaching children to

(a)   think of a range of solutions

(b)   think about the possible consequences for self and others of different actions

(c)   consider cause and effect

(d)   be sensitive to the interpersonal issues

(e)   develop means–ends thinking, that is step-by-step planning to reach a goal

(f)   encourage perspective-taking (see also the Positive Values domain).

5.   The most useful principle for this domain is the encouragement of the child to generate alternative solutions to problems. So, for example, if a child wants a toy that another child has, he or she can be asked to think of all possible actions; the adult should not make a judgement on the suggestions, rather say 'That's one idea. Can you think of another idea?' The following quote from Shure and Spivak (1978, pp.36–37, cited by Goldstein 1999), illustrates the informal application of the principles:

Four-year-old Ralph let a friend play with his racing car, but the friend has played with it a long time and Ralph has just grabbed it back.

Mother: How do you think your friend feels when you grab toys? [Encourages perspective taking]

Ralph: Mad, but I don't care, it's mine!

Mother: What did your friend do when you grabbed the toy? [Encourages cause and effect thinking]

Ralph: He hit me but I want my toy.

Mother: How did that make you feel? [Encourages emotional awareness]

Ralph: Mad.

Mother: You're mad and your friend is mad, and he hit you. Can you think of a different way to get your toy back so you both won't be mad and so John won't hit you? [Encourages alternative thinking]

Ralph: I could ask him.

Mother: And what might happen then? [Encourages consequential thinking]

Ralph: He'll say no.

Mother: He might say no. What else can you think of doing so your friend will give you back your racing car? [Encourage alternative thinking]

Ralph: I could let him have my Matchbox cars.

Mother: You thought of two different ways.

10

Case Studies

DAVID, AGED 4

Vulnerabilities and adversities

David had undiagnosed learning problems exacerbating his difficulties with peers and with his siblings. His mother was at a loss as to how to respond to him and her confusion accelerated David's ambivalent behaviour, which was a combination of neediness and anger. He was at the point of being excluded from nursery school. David has lived with his mother and siblings throughout his life but she has always had difficulty in setting limits on the four children's behaviour. She has had a succession of partners, all of whom have eventually left the family, resulting in profound confusion for David. David has developed a pattern of insecure-ambivalent attachment to his mother. His special needs, combined with her erratic limit-setting, have led to difficult behaviour in the nursery setting. His mother has a history of profound neglect and abuse. Two of his siblings, both older, have left the nuclear family to be cared for by extended family members.

Resilience and protective factors

David has a capacity to draw adults into a commitment to him. He is affectionate as well as demanding. He has a talent for construction in play. His mother, although struggling, was committed to him. The local authority found respite carers who were calm and experienced and who supported both David and his mother. A clinical psychologist was available to identify his problems more clearly and to work with him and with his mother. His maternal grandparents were committed to supporting him and his mother. He had regular contact with his separated siblings.

Interventions

SECURE BASE

A local voluntary agency runs a series of parenting groups which mother and child were able to attend. The sessions focused on building a more secure attachment as well as on behaviour management strategies. This group also included sessions for parents on *reflection* on the links between their own history and current parenting. The psychologist incorporated learning from these groups in her sessions with the mother to consolidate the attachment. The respite carers provided some relief care of David for his mother and supported her in behavioural strategies.

FRIENDSHIPS

This was the most problematic area and gradually the respite carer helped David to begin, slowly, to collaborate with one child over tasks in nursery. David now sees this child outside nursery, supported by the respite carers.

EDUCATION

The psychologist was able to clarify the precise areas of special leaning needs. She supported the nursery as well as David's mother in joint strategies for harnessing his curiosity and interest in areas of learning. Joint meetings to review strategies involving David's mother and the nursery helped to mark progress and set new goals. The male respite carer supported David in the nursery class.

TALENTS AND INTERESTS

David's ability in constructive play was deliberately encouraged and celebrated at home and in the nursery setting.

POSITIVE VALUES

David is gradually being helped to demonstrate empathy towards other children as he is feeling more secure. This is having ripple benefits for his links with other children.

SOCIAL COMPETENCIES

Some success and mastery in the nursery setting has provided a basis for an increased sense of competence, reducing David's previously acute sense of frustration.

Messages

The strengthening of his secure base of attachment relationships has been, and remains, a vital focus of joint work between David's mother and the professionals. Supports to mother in reflecting on her own history are gradually increasing her ability to be more aware of the impact of her past on her current parenting. She feels less isolated emphasising the potential of a group work approach with parents. Skilled assessment of the precise nature of David's difficulties was vital in developing effective strategies for building resilience. Effective communication between the professionals and David's mother was, and remains, crucial in assessment, goal-setting and review of strategies for work. Harnessing existing strengths in David has built self-esteem and provided a platform for the development of ripple benefits in extending his learning and strengthening links and cooperation with other children. Strategies for healing past hurts can effectively be combined with a focus on building strengths.

SUSAN, AGED 3
Vulnerabilities and adversities

Susan is an anxious child whose clingy behaviour exacerbates her mother's impatience. The past separations have increased Susan's pattern of anxious attachment. She is aggressive with peers and competitive with other children in the foster placement. Her angry, demanding clinging has led to the breakdown of a previous foster placement. Susan talks of herself as a 'bad girl' and she has low self-esteem and little confidence. Susan has significant visual problems. Susan has had a history of separations from her lone birth mother, who experiences periods of depression. When ill, her mother has been emotionally unavailable to her. Susan is currently in foster care following extreme domestic violence towards her mother. Her mother is committed to her partner and there is no possibility of a return home being in Susan's best interests. Mother's contact with Susan is erratic and her behaviour towards her is ambivalent.

Resilience and protective factors

Susan has good language skills for her age. She loves stories and has an expressive capacity. She has more secure attachments to her grandparents than to her mother. Susan now has a committed carer who cared for her on a previous removal from home. Her maternal grandparents are keen to maintain contact and support her placement away from home.

Interventions
SECURE BASE

Strategies are needed to build more secure attachments to Susan's foster carer. Deliberate work with her mother is required to regularise and supervise contact. Focused work on plans for a permanent placement should ensure predictability in the long term. Promotion of continuing links with her grandparents is focused on clear *purposes* involving:

- expressions of interest and concern

- celebration of progress and developmental gains

- continuity of links with her birth family to promote a healthy sense of identity

- permission to be in the placement and make attachments which her mother is sadly unable to give.

EDUCATION

Support in the placement for Susan's expressive capacity should help her to build a language for her feelings. Encouragement of her interest in stories is a basis for the promotion of reading skills when she starts school. A nursery placement should involve her female carer, transferring security into a learning setting. Diagnosis and treatment of her visual problems are required, and effective use of specific visual aids, using skills available at the nursery. Support to the carers should come from a worker with particular experience in work with young children with visual problems.

FRIENDSHIPS

Deliberate use of an older child in the nursery is helping Susan to settle. Strategies for supporting Susan in the group setting are needed, initially with low expectations of large group involvement.

TALENTS AND INTERESTS

Deliberate focus by carers on *feelings* should provide a basis for making some sense of past life events. Harnessing of experience and ability by the social worker in structured work would make a coherent story of her past. Use of concrete methods of work using dolls, large maps and enlarged photographs would represent past carers and specific life events.

SOCIAL COMPETENCIES

Helping Susan to use specific techniques to accommodate her visual problems will build her confidence and assertion.

Messages

Clarification of her secure base and conditions of predictability of contact with supportive adults from her past will increase the probability of supportive messages. Building the attachments in her placement will challenge her internal working model of attachments, which has left her with a preoccupation with attachment figures and low levels of healthy exploration. A realistic picture of her abilities and potential challenges an unhelpful focus on the 'disability' of her visual problems. Specialised advice *translated into practical strategies* is vital in supporting her carers to promote her potential. Clarifying the *purposes* of contact and strengthening its benefits enhance security.

Appendix

Moral Reasoning Stages

The most famous example used to assess moral reasoning is that of Kohlberg (1969, p.379).

> In Europe, a woman was near death from a very bad disease, a special kind of cancer. There was one drug that the doctors thought might save her. It was a form of radium that a druggist in the same town had recently discovered. The drug was expensive to make, but the druggist was charging ten times what the drug cost him to make. He paid $200 for the radium and charged $2,000 for a small dose of the drug. The sick woman's husband, Heinz, went to everyone he knew to borrow the money, but he could only get together about $1,000, which was half of what it cost. He told the druggist that his wife was dying, and asked him to sell it cheaper or let him pay later. But the druggist said, 'No, I discovered the drug and I'm going to make money from it.' Heinz got desperate and broke into the man's store to steal the drug for his wife.
>
> Should the husband have done that? Was it right or wrong?

It is the reasons given for the answer that were more interesting to Kohlberg than the actual answer. Table A.1 shows the stages of reasoning he found. In summary the reasons given fall into one of three broad categories (Steinberg 1993): preconventional, conventional or postconventional.

Preconventional level

Typical of younger children, up to the age of about 9, this level of reasoning focuses on rewards and punishments. There is no reference to societal rules or conventions. Justifications for actions are based upon meeting one's own interests and letting others do the same. Examples of responses at this stage (from Steinberg 1993) would be that it would be right to steal the drug 'because people would have been angry with him if he let his wife die' or that he would be wrong to because he would be put in prison.

Conventional level

This level is demonstrated from middle childhood and into adolescence and often beyond into adulthood. The focus here is more upon how others, especially significant others, will judge you. There is appeal to social rules that should be upheld. It is considered important to be a 'good' person and to demonstrate trust, loyalty, respect and gratitude. 'One behaves properly because, in so doing, one receives the approval of others and helps maintain social order.' Examples of responses here would be that he should not steal because it is against the law, or that he should steal because it is what is expected of a good husband.

Postconventional or principled level

The subject of much debate and not widely found in empirical studies, this level represents reasoning that is based upon principles of justice, fairness, the sanctity of human life and so on. It is argued to be appropriate to break the law on occasions where the law violates a fundamental principle. An example of a response would be that Heinz should not steal the drug because by doing so he violates a principle that everyone has the right to pursue a livelihood. Another example would be that he should steal because preserving life is more important than the right to make a living.

Table A.1 Kohlberg's stages of moral development

Level 1: **Preconventional** morality

Stage 1: Punishment-and-obedience orientation	What is right is whatever others permit; what is wrong is what others punish. There is no conception of rules. The seriousness of a violation depends on the magnitude of the consequence.
Stage 2: Individualism and instrumental orientation	Rules are followed only when it is in the child's immediate interest. Right is what gains rewards or when there is an equal exchange ('you scratch my back and I'll scratch yours').

Level 2: **Conventional** morality

Stage 3: Mutual interpersonal expectations, relationships, and conformity	'Being good' means living up to other people's expectations, having good intentions, and showing concern about others. Trust, loyalty, respect and gratitude are valued.
Stage 4: Social system and conscience	'Right' is a matter of fulfilling the actual duties to which you have agreed. Social rules and conventions are upheld except where they conflict with other social duties. Contributing to society is 'good'.

Level 3: **Postconventional** morality

Stage 5: Social contract or utility and individual rights	People hold a variety of values and opinions, and while rules are relative to the group these should be upheld because they are part of the social contract. Rules that are imposed are unjust and can be challenged. Some values, such as life and liberty, are non-relative and must be upheld regardless of majority opinion.
Stage 6: Universal ethical principles	Self-chosen ethical principles determine what is right. In a conflict between law and such principles, it is right to follow one's conscience. The principles are abstract moral guidelines organized into a coherent value system.

Source: Reproduced with permission from Schaffer 1996, p.295.

Bibliography

Ainsworth, M. D. S., Blehar, M., Walters, E. and Walls, S. (1978) *Patterns of Attachment*. Hillsdale, NJ: Erlbaum.

Bar-Tal, D., Raviv, A. and Goldberg, M. (1982) 'Helping behavior among pre-school children: an observational study.' *Child Development 53*, 396–402.

Benson, P. L. (1997) *All Kids are our Kids: What Communities Must Do to Raise Caring and Responsible Children and Adolescents*. San Francisco, CA: Jossey-Bass.

Bernard, B. (1991) *Fostering Resiliency in Kids: Protective Factors in the Family, School and Community*. Portland, OR: Northwest Regional Education Laboratory.

Bigelow, B. J. and La Gaipa, J. J. (1980) 'The development of friendship values and choice.' In H. C. Foot, A. J. Chapman and J. R. Smith (eds) *Friendships and Social Relations in Children*. Chichester: Wiley.

Bronfenbrenner, U. (1989) 'Ecological systems theory.' *Annals of Child Development 6*, 187–249.

Brooks, R. B. (1994) 'Children at risk: fostering resilience and hope.' *American Journal of Orthopsychiatry 64*, 4, 545–553.

Bruce, T. and Meggit, C. (1999) *Child Care and Education*. London: Hodder and Stoughton.

Buss, A. H. and Plomin, R. A. (1984) *Temperament Theory of Personality Development*. New York: Wiley-Interscience.

Chess, S. and Thomas, A. (1977) 'Temperamental individuality from childhood to adolescence.' *Journal of Child Psychiatry 16*, 218–226.

Daniel, B. M. and Taylor, J. (2001) *Engaging with Fathers: A Guide for Health and Social Care*. London: Jessica Kingsley.

Daniel, B. M., Wassell, S. and Gilligan, R. (1999) *Child Development for Child Care and Protection Workers*. London: Jessica Kingsley.

Derman-Sparks, L. (1989) *Anti-Bias Curriculum: Tools for Empowering Young Children*. Washington, DC: ABC Task Force, National Association for the Education of Young Children.

Donaldson, M. (1978) *Children's Minds*. London: Fontana.

Downes, C. (1992) *Separation Revisited: Adolescents in Foster Family Care.* Aldershot: Ashgate.

Dunn, J. (1993) *Young Children's Close Relationships: Beyond Attachment.* London: Sage.

Dunn, J. and Kendrick, C. (1982) *Siblings: Love, Envy and Understanding.* Oxford: Basil Blackwell.

Erikson, E. H. (1963) *Childhood and Society.* New York: Norton.

Fahlberg, V. I. (1991) *A Child's Journey through Placement.* London: British Agencies for Adoption and Fostering.

Feeney, J. and Noller, P. (1996) *Adult Attachment.* Thousand Oaks, CA: Sage.

Fonagy, P., Steele, M., Steele, H., Higgitt, A. and Target, M. (1994) The Emanuel Miller Memorial Lecture 1992: 'The theory and practice of resilience.' *Journal of Child Psychology and Psychiatry 35,* 2, 231–257.

Foot, H. C., Morgan, M. J. and Shute, R. H. (1990) 'Children's helping relationships: an overview.' In H. C. Foot, M. J. Morgan and R. H. Shute (eds) *Children Helping Children.* Chichester: Wiley.

Forehand, R. and McMahon, R. J. (1981) *Helping the Non-Compliant Child.* New York: Guildford.

Fox, N. A., Kimmerly, N. L. and Schafer, W. D. (1991) 'Attachment to mother/attachment to father: a meta-analysis.' *Child Development 62,* 210–225.

Freeman, N. H., Lewis, C. and Doherty, M. J. (1991) 'Preschoolers grasp of a desire for knowledge in false-belief prediction: practical intelligence and verbal report.' *British Journal of Developmental Psychology 9,* 139–157.

Garbarino, J., Dubrow, N., Kosteleny, K. and Pardo, C. (1992) *Children in Danger: Coping with the Consequences of Community Violence.* San Francisco, CA: Jossey-Bass.

Gilligan, R. (1997) 'Beyond permanence? The importance of resilience in child placement practice and planning.' *Adoption and Fostering 21,* 1, 12–20.

Gilligan, R. (1998) 'The importance of schools and teachers in child welfare.' *Child and Family Social Work 3,* 1, 13–26.

Goldstein, A. P. (1999) *The Prepare Curriculum: Teaching Prosocial Competencies.* Champaign, IL: Research Press.

Grotberg, E. (1997) 'The international resilience project.' In M. John (ed) *A Charge against Society: The Child's Right to Protection.* London: Jessica Kingsley.

Harris, P. L., Olthof, T., Meerum Terwogt, M. and Hardman, C. E. (1987) 'Children's knowledge of situations that provoke emotion.' *International Journal of Behavioural Development 10,* 319–343.

Harter, S. (1985) *The Self-Perception Profile for Children.* Denver, CO: University of Denver.

Hartup, W. W. (1992) 'Friendships and their developmental significance.' In H. McGurk (ed) *Childhood Social Development: Contemporary Perspectives.* Hove: Erlbaum.

Hinde, R. A., Titmus, G., Easton, D. and Tamplin, A. (1985) 'Incidence of "friendship" and behavior with strong associates versus non-associates in preschoolers.' *Child Development 56,* 234–245.

Holmes, J. (1993) 'Attachment theory: a biological basis for psychotherapy.' *British Journal of Psychiatry 163,* 430–438.

Howe, D. (1995) *Attachment Theory for Social Work Practice.* London: Macmillan.

Howe, D., Brandon, M., Hinings, D. and Schofield, G. (1999) *Attachment Theory, Child Maltreatment and Family Support.* London: Macmillan.

Kohlberg, L. (1969) 'Stages and sequence: the cognitive-developmental approach to socialization.' In D. A. Goslin (ed) *Handbook of Socialization Theory and Research.* Chicago: Rand McNally.

Lewis, C. and Osborne, A. (1990) 'Three-year-olds' problems with false belief: conceptual deficit or linguistic artifact?' *Child Development 61,* 1514–1519.

Luthar, S. S. (1991) 'Vulnerability and resilience: a study of high-risk adolescents.' *Child Development 62,* 600–612.

McClellan, D. E. and Katz, L. G. (1992) 'Assessing the social development of young children: a checklist of social attributes.' *Dimensions of Early Childhood 21,* 1, 9–10.

Main, M. and Weston, D. R. (1981) 'The quality of the toddler's relationship to mother and to father: related to conflict behaviour and the readiness to establish new relationships.' *Child Development 52,* 932–994.

Masten, A. (1994) 'Resilience in individual development.' In M. C. Wang and E. W. Gordon (eds) *Educational Resilience in Inner-City America.* Hillsdale, NJ: Erlbaum.

Masten, A. S. and Coatsworth, J. D. (1998) 'The development of competence in favorable and unfavorable environments.' *American Psychologist 53,* 2, 205–220.

Open University (1997) *Confident Parents: Confident Children.* Milton Keynes: School of Health and Social Welfare, The Open University.

Parker, R., Ward, H., Jackson, S., Aldgate, J. and Wedge, P. (1991) *Looking after Children: Assessing Outcomes in Child Care.* London: HMSO.

Perner, J., Leekam, S. R. and Wimmer, H. (1987) 'Three-year-olds' difficulty with false belief: the case for a conceptual deficit.' *British Journal of Developmental Psychology 5,* 125–137.

Petersen, C. and Seligman, M. E. P. (1985) 'The learned helplessness model of depression: current status of theory and research.' In E. Beckham (ed) *Handbook of Depression: Treatment, Assessment and Research.* Homewood, IL: Dorsey Press.

Piaget, J. (1952) *The Origins of Intelligence in Children.* New York: International Universities Press.

Promoting Social Competence (1999) University of Dundee and the Scottish Executive. http://www.dundee.ac.uk/psychology/prosoc.htm.

Raundalen, M. (1991) *Care and Courage.* Sweden: Rädda Barnen.

Rutter, M. (1985) 'Resilience in the face of adversity: protective factors and resistance to psychiatric disorder.' *British Journal of Psychiatry 147,* 598–611.

Rutter, M. (1991) 'Pathways from childhood to adult life: the role of schooling.' *Pastoral Care,* September, 3–10.

Santrok, J. W. (1994) *Child Development.* Madison, WI and Dubuque, IA: W. C. B. Brown and Benchmark.

Schaffer, H. R. (1996) *Social Development.* Oxford: Blackwell.

Schaffer, H. R. and Emerson, P. E. (1964) 'The development of social attachments in infancy.' *Monographs of the Society for Research in Child Development, 29*, 3, (whole no. 94).

Shure, M. B. and Spivak, G. (1978) *Problem-Solving Techniques in Childrearing.* San Francisco, CA: Jossey-Bass.

Smith, P. K. and Cowie, H. (1991) *Understanding Children's Development.* Oxford: Blackwell.

Spivak, G. and Shure, M. B. (1974) *Social Adjustment of Young Children.* San Francisco: Jossey-Bass.

Steinberg, L. (1993) *Adolescence.* New York: McGraw-Hill.

Terwogt, M. M. and Stegge, H. (1998) 'Children's perspective on the emotional process.' In A. Campbell and S. Mincer (eds) *The Social Child.* Hove: Psychology Press.

Thompson, R. A. (1995) *Preventing Child Maltreatment Through Social Support.* Thousand Oaks, CA: Sage.

Vygotsky, L. S. (1962) *Thought and Language.* Cambridge, MA: MIT Press.

Werner, E. (1990) 'Protective factors and individual resilience.' In S. Meisels and J. Shonkoff (eds) *Handbook of Early Childhood Intervention.* Cambridge: Cambridge University Press.

Werner, E. E. and Smith, R. S. (1992) *Overcoming the Odds: High Risk Children from Birth to Adulthood.* Ithaca, NY: Cornell University Press.

Willow, C. and Hoyder, T. (1998) *It Hurts You Inside.* London: Save the Children and National Children's Bureau.

Zahn-Waxler, C., Radke-Yarrow, M. and King, R. A. (1979) 'Child-rearing and children's prosocial initiations towards victims of distress.' *Child Development 50*, 319–330.

Subject Index

actively reaching for others 15
adaptability 16
addiction problems 16
adversities 11, 119, 121
affectionate 15
aggression 74
alertness 16
altruism 43
ambivalent attachment (Type C) 28, 34
angry face 62, 63
angry scene 67, 69
Anti-Bias Curriculum: Tools for Empowering Young Children (Derman-Sparks) 113
anxious preoccupation 28
appearance 50
assessment 20, 25–81
    and intervention chart 21, 22–3
athletic competence 50
attachment
    ambivalent 28
    avoidant 27, 28
    disorganised 28
    network
        wider resources contributing to child's 31, 33
            capitalising upon 93–6
    quality of 34
    secure and insecure 15, 27–9
    sibling 16
attention 76, 81, 115–16
attributes
    individual 78
    peer relationship 79
    social skills 78–9
    see also Social Attributes Checklist
attributions 73
autonomy 75, 80, 114
avoidant attachment (Type A) 27, 28, 34

balancing act 85–6
behavioural conduct 50
behavioural development 15
birth complications, lack of 15
British Agencies for Adoption and Fostering (BAAF) 7

care-giving 57
    empathic 58
case studies 119–23
    interventions 120, 122–3

messages 121, 123
    resilience and protective factors 119, 121–2
    vulnerabilities and adversities 119, 121
Center for Sexual Assault and Traumatic Stress, Harborview Medical Center, Seattle 34
Centre for Child Care and Protection Studies, Dundee University 7
cheerfulness 16
Child Care and Education (Bruce and Meggit) 113
child checklist 19
children, four or fewer 16
Children's Centres, North Edinburgh 7
Children's Research Centre, Trinity College, Dublin 7
close bond with at least one person 16
cognitive development of child
    extent that parent/carer environment facilitates 38–9, 40–1
    helping enhance parent/carer environment to facilitate 98–100
    wider opportunities for 39, 41
        exploring 100–1
cognitive skills 35
comforting behaviour
    encouraging child to show 112–13
    level of shown by child 61, 71
communication, advanced in 16
community, wider 9
competence 15
    athletic 50
    scholastic 50
Confident Parents: Confident Children (Open University) 113
conflict management/resolution, social skills in 43
conformity 126
conscience and social system 126
continuity of opportunity 51
conventional level of moral reasoning 125, 126
cooperative play, poor social skills in 43
curiosity about child's environment
    extent of 38, 40
    helping development of 97–8

dimension on which resilience can be located 11
disorganised attachment (Type D) 28, 34
drive and vigour 15
Dundee University 7, 72

ecological approach to intervention 86
ecological framework 9–10
ecological levels at which resilience factors can be located 9
education 14, 15, 18, 22, 35–41
    background information 35–7
    checklists
        child 38–9

parent/carer 40–1
interventions 86, 120, 122
practice suggestions for intervention
strategies 97–101
emotional development 15
emotional faces 62–3
emotional problems 43
emotional scenes 65–9
emotional support 43
empathy 58
of children with people close to them,
helping 110–11
ethical principles, universal 126
evaluation 21

family
factors associated with resilience 16
harmony 16
relationships 9, 10, 15
fearlessness 16
feeding, easy 15
feelings, helping child to understand own
110–11
female 15
financial and material resources, sufficient 16
first-born 15
friend(ship)s 14, 15, 18, 23, 42–8, 72, 86
background information 42–4
characteristics to help make and keep friends
45, 47
helping child to develop 102–3
checklists
child 47–8
parent/carer 47–8
close bond of 16
helping child's current 104
interventions 120, 122
parent/carer environment facilitates
development of
encouraging 103
extent 46, 47–8
practice suggestions for intervention
strategies 102–4
what are child's friendships like at moment?
45, 48
frightened face 62, 63
frightened scene 65, 69
full term 15
future, sense of 72

grandparents, close 16
group entry, poor social skills in 43
group play 44

happy face 62, 63
happy scene 66, 69

health 15
helpful behaviour
encouraging child to help others 111–12
extent of child's 60–1, 70
holistic approach to intervention 86

identity 15
immature perspective-taking ability 43
individual 10
individual attributes 78
individual rights 126
individualism and instrumental orientation 126
insecure attachment 27–9
ambivalent (Type C) 28, 34
avoidant (Type A) 27, 28, 34
disorganised (Type D) 28, 34
internal locus of control 72
International Resilience Project 12
intervention 20, 83–118
balancing act 85–6
case studies 120, 122–3
ecological approach 86
holistic approach 86
introduction 85
multi-agency, network approach 86–7
practice suggestions
education 97–101
friendships 102–4
positive values 110–13
secure base 87–96
social competencies 113–18
talents and interests 104–9
process of assessment and planning for 17
strategies 85–118
intimate relationships 43
It Hurts You Inside (Willow and Hoyder) 113

Kohlberg's stages of moral development 7,
124–6

LAC (Looking After Children) materials 15, 17,
20

Maryhill Social Work Centre, Glasgow 7
mental health, lack of parental 16
moral development, Kohlberg's stages of 124–6
moral reasoning 56
helping child develop 110–11
stages 124–6
conventional level 125, 126
postconventional or principled level 125,
126
preconventional level 124, 126
multi-agency, network approach to intervention
86–7

mutual interpersonal expectations 126

neighbour and other non-kin support 16
network approach to intervention 86–7
novel experiences, seeking out 16
nursery experience, good 16
nurturance 16

opportunity, continuity of 51

parallel play 44
parent/carer checklist 20
peer
    contact 16
    relationship(s) 15
        attributes 79
personal characteristics, extent of contribution to
    child's level of social competence 75–6,
    80–1
perspective, ability to see others' 60, 70
Perth Social Work Department 7
physical appearance 50
play 44
positive values 14, 15, 19, 23, 56–71, 72, 86
    background information 56–9
    checklists
        child 60–1
        parent/carer 70–1
    interventions 120
    practice suggestions for intervention
        strategies 110–13
postconventional level of moral reasoning 125,
    126
practice suggestions for intervention strategies
    education 97–101
    friendships 102–4
    positive values 110–13
    secure base 87–96
    social competencies 113–18
    talents and interests 104–9
preconventional level of moral reasoning 56,
    124, 126
principled level of moral reasoning 125, 126
problem-solving 72
'Promoting Social Competence' project 72
prosocial behaviour 56–8
    encouraging child to show 112–13
    modelling by significant adults 57–8
protective environment 11
protective factors, resilience and 119, 121–2
punishment-and-obedience orientation 126
purpose, sense of 72

quality of attachment 34

relationships
    family 9, 15
    intimate 43
    mutual interpersonal expectations,
        conformity and 126
    peer 15
resilience 10–14, 42, 72
    dimension on which resilience can be
        located 11
    domains of 14–15
    during early years, summary of factors
        associated with 15–16
    ecological framework 9–10
    family factors associated with 16
    framework for assessment of factors 11
    individual factors associated with 15–16
    introduction to 9–16
    and protective factors 119, 121–2
    wider community factors associated with 16

sad face 62, 63
sad scene 68, 69
scaffolding 36
scholastic competence 50
school or college
    poor adjustment 43
    poor attainment 43
Scottish Executive 7, 72
secure attachment (Type B) 15, 27–9, 34
secure base 14, 15, 18, 22, 27–34
    background information 27–9
    checklists
        child 30–1
        parent/carer 32–3
    of child 30, 32
    ensuring child has 91–3
    helping child feel secure 89–90
    interventions 86, 120, 122
    practice suggestions for intervention
        strategies 87–96
    provided by parent/carer environment 31,
        32–3
    quality of attachment 34
self-care 15
self-control 75, 80, 114
self-efficacy 76, 80, 115
self-esteem 35, 49, 58
self-knowledge 42
separations, lack of 16
sharing behaviour
    encouraging child to show 112–13
    level of shown by child 61, 71
sibling attachment 16
sleeping, easy 15
sociability 43
social acceptance 50

Social Attributes Checklist (McClellan and Katz) 75, 78–9
social competence(s) 14, 15, 19, 23, 49, 72–81
  background information 72–4
  checklists
    child 75–7
    parent/carer 80–1
  encouragement of by parent/carer
    environment 76, 81
    helping 116
  helping child to develop, in wider social
    environment 116–18
  helping child to develop personal
    characteristics that help with 113–16
  interventions 86, 120, 123
  opportunities to develop in wider social
    environment 76, 81
  personal characteristics as contribution to
    child's level of 75–6, 80–1
  practice suggestions for intervention
    strategies 113–18
  Social Attributes Checklist 75, 78–9
  social contract or utility and individual
    rights 126
social presentation 15
social skills 42, 44
  attributes 78–9
  poor 43
social system and conscience 126
Social Work Services Inspectorate, Scottish
  Executive 7
socially responsive behaviour 15
solitary play 44
stress 43

talents and interests 14, 15, 19, 23, 49–55
  background information 49–51
  checklists
    child 52–3
    parent/carer 54–5
  of child 52, 54
    encouraging 105–7
  development/expression of encouraged by
    parent/carer environment 53, 54–5
    ensuring 107–8
  intervention 86, 120, 122–3
  opportunities in wider environment for
    nurturing 53, 55
    drawing upon 109
  practice suggestions for intervention
    strategies 104–9
temperament 76, 80, 114
theory of mind 57, 64
Trinity College, Dublin 7
trust 16

understanding of own feelings, helping child
  110–11
universal ethical principles 126

values, positive see positive values
vigour 15
vulnerabilities 11, 119, 121

wider community 9, 10
  factors associated with resilience 16
workbook, when and how to use 17–23
  assessment 20
  child checklist 19
  evaluation 21
  how? 18–19
  intervention 20
  parent/carer checklist 20
  when? 17–18

Author Index

Ainsworth, M.D.S. 27, 127
Aldgate, J. 129

Bar-Tal, D. 57, 127
Beckham, E. 129
Benson, P.L. 56, 127
Berliner, L. 32, 34
Bernard, B. 72, 127
Bigelow, B.J. 44, 127
Blehar, M. 127
Brandon, M. 129
Bronfenbrenner, U. 9, 127
Brooks, R.B. 49, 51, 127
Bruce, T. 113, 127
Buss, A.H. 114, 127

California State Department of Education 49
Chapman, A.J. 127
Chess, S. 114, 127
Coatsworth, J.D. 73, 74
Cowie, H. 36, 44, 57, 64, 130

Daniel, B.M. 7, 11, 27, 97, 127
Derman-Sparks, L. 113, 127
Doherty, M.J. 64, 128
Donaldson, M. 35, 127
Downes, C. 28, 128
Dubrow, N. 128
Dunn, J. 58, 89, 128

Easton, D. 128
Emerson, P.E. 49, 130
Ennis, E. 7
Ennis, J. 7
Erikson, E.H. 73, 128

Fahlberg, V.I. 27, 90, 128
Feeney, J. 29, 128
Fine, D. 32, 34
Fonagy, P. 10, 29, 128
Foot, H.C. 42, 127, 128
Forehand, R. 107, 128
Fox, N.A. 29, 128
Freeman, N.H. 64, 128

Garbarino, J. 35, 128
Gilligan, R. 7, 11, 12, 13, 35, 127, 128

Goldberg, M. 57, 127
Goldstein, A.P. 117, 128
Goslin, D.A. 129
Grotberg, E. 12, 86, 87, 128

Hardman, C.E. 128
Harris, P.L. 57, 128
Harter, S. 49, 50, 128
Hartup, W.W. 42, 128
Henderson, C. 7
Higgitt, A. 128
Hinde, R.A. 44, 128
Hinings, D. 129
Holmes, J. 43, 128
Howe, D. 27, 28, 30, 43, 129
Hoyder, T. 113, 130

Jackson, S. 129
John, M. 128

Katz, L.G. 75, 78, 129
Kendrick, C. 58, 128
Kimmerly, N.L. 29, 128
King, R.A. 57, 130
Kohlberg, L. 7, 56, 124, 125, 129
Kosteleny, K. 128

La Gaipa, J.J. 44, 127
Leekam, S.R. 64, 129
Lewis, C. 64, 128, 129
Luthar, S.S. 12, 49, 72, 129

McClellan, D.E. 75, 78, 129
McMahon, R.J. 107, 128
Main, M. 29, 129
Masten, A.S. 73, 74, 85, 129
Meggit, C. 113, 127
Meisels, S. 130
Morgan, M.J. 42, 128

Noller, P. 29, 128

Olthof, T. 128
Open University 113, 129
Osborne, A. 64, 129

Pardo, C. 128
Parker, R. 15, 129
Perner, J. 64, 129
Petersen, C. 73, 129
Piaget, J. 35, 129
Plomin, R.A. 114, 127

Promoting Social Competence 72, 129

Radke-Yarrow, M. 57, 130
Raundalen, M. 56, 58, 129
Raviv, A. 57, 127
Rutter, M. 10, 35, 129

Santrok, J.W. 114, 129
Schafer, W.D. 29, 128
Schaffer, H.R. 7, 42, 43, 44, 49, 57, 74, 126,
    129, 130
Schofield, G. 129
Seligman, M.E.P. 73, 129
Shonkoff, J. 130
Shure, M.B. 117, 130
Shute, R.H. 42, 128
Smith, J.R. 127
Smith, P.K. 36, 44, 56, 57, 64, 130
Smith, R.S. 11, 56, 72, 130
Spivak, G. 117, 130
Steele, H. 128
Steele, M. 128
Stegge, H. 57, 130
Steinberg, L. 124, 130

Tamplin, A. 128
Target, M. 128
Taylor, J. 97, 127
Terwogt, M.M. 57, 128, 130
Thomas, A. 114, 127
Thompson, R.A. 42, 43, 44, 94, 130
Titmus, G. 128

Vygotsky, L.S. 36, 130

Walls, S. 127
Walters, E. 127
Ward, H. 129
Wassell, S. 7, 11, 127
Wedge, P. 129
Werner, E. 11, 27, 42, 56, 72, 130
Weston, D.R. 29, 129
Willow, C. 113, 130
Willshaw, D. 7
Wilson, A. 7
Wimmer, H. 64, 129
Wosu, H. 7

Zahn-Waxler, C. 57, 130